Investing in
# Student Housing
in Hamilton, Ontario, Canada

by

Robert J. Morrow

*Other books by Robert J. Morrow:*

**Sold Strategies** *(US & Canada Edition)*
The Cheapest, Safest, and Smartest Ways to Sell Your Home!*
(Copyright 2016, Sunao International)

**Buck Tradition**
The Smartest Way to SELL YOUR HOME in Canada*
(Copyright 2014, Sunao International)

**The Barre Chord Approach**
Learn to Play Guitar in 30 Days!*
(Copyright 1993, Vandine Group)

**25 Years of Magic**
Corporate biography of Matsushita Electric of Canada Ltd (1967-1992)
(Copyright 1992, Panasonic Canada)

*available at www.amazon.ca and www.amazon.com
in paperback and Kindle version,
or at: www.robertjmorrow.com

ISBN# 13: 978-1536947328    10: 1536947326

***Morrow, R.J. 1957-***
***First Edition September 2016 (trade paperback and e-book)***

sunao

*To my son, Jared, who was attending University during the writing of this book.*
*He managed to ensure all the issues were kept top of mind.*

# Table of Contents

Student Housing

# About this book

For many, Hamilton, Ontario is the City of choice when considering Student Housing in Canada. Of course there is student housing in many cities across Canada, but none have shown the consistent ROI numbers that Hamilton (and the surrounding area) has. Other municipalities have interfered with university/investor relations and, as a result, have driven investors out of their markets with their bylaws and restrictions (Waterloo and Vancouver). Others are simply in too highly-priced neighbourhoods (York, University of Toronto, University of British Columbia, etc.). And still others are, at time of print, too small to warrant wide-spread interest (scores of community colleges in every province). But also at time of print, there were several emerging markets that show potential (two of which are discussed in this book that are close enough to Hamilton to be worthy of consideration: St. Catharines and Brantford).

Hamilton hit the top of the roster when the Financial Times officially listed the steel town as the #1 City in Canada for investing in 2011. This launched an interest, nationwide, from all kinds of investors looking for all kinds of vehicles. From duplexes and triplexes (of which Hamilton has an abundance), to multi-level, multi-tenant apartment buildings. When Ontario passed legislation shortly thereafter, allowing owners of residential homes in suburbs to build legal apartments in their basement, the *Second Suite* phenomenon began and Hamilton became a leader in the retro-fitting of bungalows into legal as well as non-conforming duplexes. And when the City lost its bid to license student housing in 2014, Hamilton became one of only a handful of thriving university municipalities with workable rules and regulations as it pertained to student home investing.

At the turn of the century student housing was a flourishing investment vehicle but wasn't well known. Most of the existing student residence investors were parents of children attending McMaster University, or locals who had recognized the opportunity early on.

But it didn't take long for the savvy investor--especially those in the lower price ranges (<$300,000) to realize that with a combination of steady cash flow and a high resale value, this was a higher range ROI real estate investment. By 2000, market prices had risen and properties that had been held since the early 1980s were now being offered up for sale again... en masse. Locals were cashing out and out-of-town investors were catching the wave.

Since that time, many out-of-town investors have profited greatly both from a steady, above-average cash flow, and a high ROI upon sale of the property. On average, investors hold properties for five to ten years and experience a 6-10% annual ROI (some even higher) when assessing the combined cash flow and profit from sale. Much of the profit is garnered from appreciation and since this is not a factor used by 99.9% of real estate investors, student housing continues to thrive under the radar.

Student home prices have risen a minimum of 10% per year for the past decade and sales of these homes are still stronger than ever. This is, in part, due to the growth of McMaster University and its continued expansion into other sectors of the City. There is a continued need for more accommodations for students but there has not been a corresponding growth in new building development, and certainly no new student residences. I received a letter in early 2016 asking me to advise landlords that there was an abundance of foreign and first year students for the 2016/2017 semester and accommodations were going to be one of the major concerns for the university. They were begging my clients to advertise their properties on the university website in order for these new students to finalize rooms up to eight months in advance.

Much of continued need for housing is the result of a City Council that continues to struggle with the concept, despite it being the elephant in the room. And so, in order to meet the needs of the University, residences that are sold within a 2-mile radius of the main campus are almost always reverted into student homes. At the turn of the century, the density of student homes to residences in the Westdale/Ainslie neighbourhoods (within 2 miles of campus) was roughly 50%. Today, it is 80% or higher.

The anomaly to all of this steady and seemingly secure income is that student housing is technically illegal. That is to say that, according to both Federal and Provincial law, there is no such housing category as "student residence". The nearest category is "lodging house" which is the closest vehicle to a student residence but with several important differences. A lodging house consists of renters signing individual leases for individual rooms or suites or even small studio-style apartments, which they are allowed to lock when not in residence. Often, lodging home tenants share kitchens and even bathrooms, but rarely a common area. Each residence adheres to fire code and is completely cut off from other residences within the same building.

A student house, on the other hand, consists of rooms that students rent in a residential environment, and is categorized as *single family residential*. Students are technically not allowed to lock their doors (though many residences allow it; the owner of the home having a copy of each room's key for emergencies). They share the kitchen, bathrooms and common areas and are, in fact, living as a single family. The distinction is that the tenants all sign one lease thereby complying with the ruling that a "single family residence be occupied by one family". By signing one lease, all the students (whether related or not) are becoming a family and are living as such in the home. By ensuring every tenant has access to every room in the home (above and below grade), the student residence is, in fact, a *single family residence.*

Despite making uninformed investors nervous, this anomaly has been in place for decades. Although several City bylaws restrict the number of tenants in single family homes and dictate the number of parking spots required, they have rarely been enforced and only when the safety of the tenants was evident. Of course, when dealing with *slum lords* the City has the bylaws in place to quickly eradicate irresponsible landlords and they have been known to enforce compliance upon said landlords. But for the most part, there is a mutual understanding that since student housing is needed, and investors are willing to spend money on repairing, renovating, and improving homes in the area, then it is good for the City and will be allowed to flourish.

Permits allowing investors to renovate and improve student homes are readily granted, despite the *official* stance being that there is no such thing as student housing. Ironically, if you call City Hall on any given day and ask if student housing is allowed in the City, the official answer will be "No". Yet the Building Department regularly approves requests for renovations that are blatantly changing three bedroom residences into eight to ten-bedroom student homes.

This book, therefore, discusses not only the opportunities available for investors, but also the do's and don'ts of navigating and, indeed, manipulating the City's regulations and requirements as it relates to student housing.

In the end, should you choose to invest, you'll have all the tools you need to do it properly, ensure a decent ROI, and be happy with the knowledge that you played a small role in shaping the future leaders of tomorrow.

# Chapter One:

# The City, the School, the Concept of Student Housing

Hamilton is situated on the farthest western point of Lake Ontario, just one hour from the US to the South-East and one hour North-West to Toronto, the nation's finance capital.

Although best known for its steel industry which peaked in the 1950s and 60s, Hamilton today is more of a health and technology city, boasting some of the most prominent health facilities and national technology leaders within its city limits. The City amalgamated with several outlying towns and villages in the 1990s and instantly increased in population to become a leading Canadian city. The towns and villages of Dundas, Ancaster, Stoney Creek, Flamborough, and Waterdown all became part of Hamilton, virtually doubling its geographic footprint around the edge of Burlington Bay.

The base City consists of a lower town following the edge of the Lake and an upper town located on the Niagara Escarpment. The upper portion is mostly residential and has plenty of room to expand southward toward Lake Erie. Mohawk College is located at the far West end of the escarpment (just before Ancaster) and some out-of-town students live within one or two blocks of the campus in investor homes.

The lower portion is typical of most large Canadian cities; namely that it has a languishing downtown core, a large lower-class neighbourhood, and several pockets of neighbourhoods where revitalization is occurring. Most of the new construction is taking place on the southern upper escarpment or in the outlying amalgamated towns of Ancaster, Stoney Creek and Waterdown. Revitalized areas include the North End (where the steel factories reside on the water's edge), portions of each amalgamated town's main street segments, and areas surrounding the four major hospitals (General, Juravinski, St. Josephs, and McMaster Children's) and the three major educational institutions (McMaster, Mohawk, and Columbia).

McMaster University is located in the west end, nestled between the escarpment to the south, the lake to the north, the town of Dundas to the West, and the main arterial highway (403) to the east, beyond which lies the downtown. Columbia College, a specialized boarding school attracting international students, is located virtually across the street from McMaster. The three learning institutions provide Hamilton with a diverse educational mix which serves not only international and national needs but more importantly, the various local communities. Hamilton boasts one of the highest percentages of students who come from elsewhere but, upon graduation, choose to stay. These transplanted residents live and work in Hamilton, usually in the health, education, or technology industries. McMaster University takes much of the credit for this, partly due to its close association with Hamilton Health Sciences (the largest medical corporation in the area) and Innovation Park (a breeding ground for emerging technology-based companies).

This book focuses primarily on students attending McMaster University, as these are students who will spend upwards of four to six years studying here and have the additional strong possibility of becoming residents upon graduation. Mohawk College, being a community institution, tends to cater to the local population and, as such, does not have as large an impact on student housing as its university counterpart. Columbia College has built a large residence for its students, most of whom come from overseas for short periods of time, returning to their homeland upon completion. There is some minor overlap into the McMaster student housing zone due to its proximity, but for the most part Columbia students stay either in residence, with family friends, or in one of the two apartment buildings directly adjacent to the college.

## McMaster University

Established in 1887 in Toronto, the University is named after Senator William McMaster (1811-1887) who bequeathed substantial funds to endow a university. In 1930, the University moved to Hamilton and the forty-first academic session opened on the present site. During the 1950s and 60s, doctoral programmes in Science and Engineering, and shortly thereafter, Humanities and Social Studies reflected the University's growing strength in research and advanced studies.

The school is currently divided into six faculties: Business, Engineering, Humanities, Science, Social Sciences, and Health Sciences (which comprises the School of Medicine, the School of Nursing, and the School of Rehabilitation Science), as well as a Faculty of Theology. McMaster also offers a wide range of part-time degree and non-degree programmes, thereby providing an additional service to members of the community who are unable to devote themselves to full-time studies. There are over forty-seven buildings providing classrooms, laboratories, seminar rooms, libraries, physical education facilities, and administrative and faculty offices, all located to the West of Westdale Village, a small and quaint inner-community that has a mandate of connecting students with the surrounding community. Some of the City's most expensive real estate is located here, and long-term residents pride themselves in being a part of the ever-changing student community evolving around them. The Royal Botanical Gardens--a private and protected portion of undeveloped natural land-- is directly adjacent to the school grounds, attracting tourists, locals, and students alike to a plethora of walking trails, canoeing and kayaking havens, and even a nationally-renowned Aviary.

## Off Campus Housing

Most universities provide some sort of assistance for students to find accommodations. First year's concentrate on getting into residence for the most part, but McMaster, like most Canadian universities simply cannot accommodate the entire student population each and every year. Many, McMaster included, utilize a lottery format for choosing those who will be invited to stay in residence. In McMaster's case, this is only offered in the first year. For second year and beyond, the students must find their own accommodations. Thus the importance of the Off-Campus Housing Desk.

McMaster boasts a strong off-campus housing operation. Though the school does not get involved in any specific housing facilities, it is pro-active in providing an up-to-date, active website where students can locate and contact landlords and arrange accommodations. The desk cannot dictate terms or pricing, nor does it inspect, or rate facilities, but it certainly influences the decision by informing students what is fair, what they can expect, and what the law says about the landlord/tenant relationship. McMaster holds regular landlord meetings, on campus, where landlords can ascertain the school's expectations as well as provide informative sessions on such things as fire prevention, local zoning information, health concerns (such as bed bug control, rodent control, etc.), and reinforce the Ontario Landlord-Tenant Act which is the basis for all rulings on landlord and tenant relationships.

That website URL is: **http://macoffcampus.mcmaster.ca**

The local Renters Association and Real Estate Board are actively involved in McMaster's off-campus housing and have been strong advocates for fair and logical administration of rental facilities in the City. For example, in 2014, City Council voted to veto licensing of student housing based primarily on information presented by these associations. Hamilton is now one of the few University cities in the country that does not demand licensing of student accommodations. Despite some critics feeling this does not allow the City to control and administrate student housing, those closely associated with the cottage industry (landlords, REALTORS®, students, faculty) recognize that by allowing self-governing, the concept of student housing in Hamilton is able to flourish and remain both affordable for the student and lucrative for the conscientious investor.

# Reno's vs turnkey

As the communities surrounding McMaster changed in the 1950s and beyond, the cry from residents that the student population density would soon reach 50% became a concern to the City. Investors began knocking down wartime homes to the South of Main Street and West of Cootes Paradise (across from the School) and began building multi-level, multi-room buildings that could only be viewed as lodging houses. Most contained 10-12 rooms on three, sometimes four floors (including the basement) and were built specifically and exclusively for students. They had no architecturally-appealing quality but were, instead, square boxes towering into the sky, directly adjacent to bungalows and one and a half storeys built fifty years prior.

## The Monster By-Law

In an ongoing effort to restrict the building of such homes, in 1995, the City enacted the Zoning by-law 95-02. Called the "Monster Home Bylaw", it effectively removed the ability to build over-sized homes based on height, lot coverage, floor area ratios, parking requirements, landscaping, and maximum bedroom limits, all by-laws already in existence. In 2005, the City addressed the issue once again in an attempt to consider rezoning in areas surrounding McMaster and Mohawk but to date, no such change has occurred. When the City of Hamilton amalgamated in 2001, each municipality had its own interpretation of zoning allowances and since then, the piecemeal zoning makes it impossible to apply one standard across the board.

Currently, the monster-home bylaw in the Ainslie-Woods area (near McMaster) enforces a gross floor area, including basement, of no more than 45 per cent of the lot size. Height is limited to two storeys. Other communities within the City have different ratio restrictions but they are based on the desire for large luxury home builds.

Over the years, primarily due to the above restrictions, homes in the Ainslie Woods/Westdale area have remained as originally built...on the outside. On the inside, however, a large number of former single family homes have been renovated to accommodate anywhere from six to ten students. By skirting around controversial and un-enforceable bylaws such as limiting number of rooms, parking, etc., these homes are successful student residences. Although there are no updated statistics to verify, many involved believe the density of student homes to single family residences now exceeds 80% in the two-mile area surrounding McMaster University.

These homes are considered turnkey, meaning when purchased, they come complete with tenants and all renovations have been accomplished to safely house said tenants. The key word there is "safely" and the one aspect the City focuses on. Many of the *compliance blitzes* that have taken place over the years were designed to remove slum landlords: those who do not repair, update, or maintain their student residences and therefore, over time, allow them to become unsafe.

## The Turnkey Home

When buying a turnkey home, your best friend will be your real estate agent. Make sure you choose one who is well versed in the nuances of student housing. Any Hamilton real estate agent will sell you a student home but only a handful attend all the Council meetings and even fewer attend the McMaster Landlord meetings held regularly at the school. These are the agents you need to steer you through the legal maze that constitutes *acceptable student housing* as an investment. The good ones know all the bylaws and all the school recommendations. They also are familiar with the school's process of providing off-campus housing to students and are invaluable for assisting you in obtaining your first group of tenants.

Usually, when buying a home that is already a successful student house, the tenants come with the deal. Although most investors do not purchase a home with a commercial mortgage (allowing leases to be considered income), the value of the leases does have an impact on the selling price. Sometimes a home is sold vacant. It has been a student home in the past but the owner, for whatever reason, has not filled it with tenants this term. This often happens with out-of-town owners who simply cannot spare the time it takes to continually tenant student homes (more on that later).

As an investor, your concern then becomes: "How soon will I be able to fill the house and begin receiving a return on my investment?" School semesters run all year long but the majority of students are in classes from Sept to the following April. The idea, therefore, is to have your home full as of Sept 1st with a twelve-month lease continuing to the next September. A large majority of home owners manage to accomplish this but there are some-again, usually out-of-towners, who do not have the time to ensure all tenants sign twelve-month leases. These landlords will often sign up tenants from Sept to April, leaving the house empty for the summer months. Sometimes, they can fill a few rooms with students attending summer courses, but usually not for full price and not for the full four months prior to September.

This dictates, therefore, when you close on a home. Not purchase, close. You can buy a student home anytime throughout the year; there is always a minimum of fifteen or so properties at any given time of year available for various reasons. But, if you want the home to make money right from day one, you need to either have it fully tenanted or be in the position to tenant it quickly. For the most part, students begin looking for accommodations in February and March each year for the May (summer) session, and July and August for the Winter semester. If you're buying an empty student house, therefore, you should be purchasing in January or June ideally. You can certainly fill up a house in April and August with latecomers, procrastinators and those first years who receive their acceptance letters late. However, it is difficult to stick to your guns about rental price when the pool of students is considerably smaller than the norm. Tenanting is a subject warranting its own discussion, so more on that later.

If the home you are purchasing states it is fully tenanted, be sure to add a clause in your offer that allows you to view the leases and verify what is stated. It is not uncommon for a seller to embellish his income (as exact numbers are not a legal requirement of a listing unless stated as such in a formal Profit and Loss Statement).

You must also remember that you are often dealing with tenants who still think like children, not responsible adults. Often, when a house is sold, the students see this as an opportunity to break their lease and move out. They don't necessarily inform the owner but on the day you close, you may find fewer tenants than you anticipated. And as mentioned above, if you purchased the house half way through a semester, the odds of finding new tenants are slim until the next semester.

One way to ensure the leases are legitimate and that the tenants intend to stay is to provide a form to each tenant asking them to verify their lease agreement and a signature verifying they are staying when you take over. This is perfectly legal and can be achieved during the *condition* stage of purchase. In most cases, the *condition* stage is the five to seven-day period during which you are obtaining financing, performing an inspection, etc., prior to waiving all conditions of the sale. (Again, more on that later). This gives you that period to meet the tenants and ensure they are staying and paying what the leases state. If you find discrepancies, you can alter the agreement accordingly via an Amendment to the Purchase of Sale Agreement, or at the very worse, have your lawyer hold back funds during the transaction that account for the discrepancy.

There are some legal loopholes to be aware of here and we'll go into more detail in the section on *making an offer* in Chapter Two.

## The Reno

If you find a residential home in the Ainslie Woods/Westdale area that hasn't already been retrofitted to be a student home, consider yourself lucky; they are far and few between. In areas of Westdale, the homes that still remain as residences are some of the larger, more luxurious homes originally built for the steel industry executives. As a result, they are some of the most expensive. On the bright side, many of them can be turned into residences that house eight to ten students, making them viable.

Other homes south of Main Street (Ainslie Woods) are not as expensive but are also smaller. When they come up, they are often reno'd to become student homes with four to six rooms available. Despite the lower price it is difficult to justify the investment when there less rooms to rent. Many of these homes are purchased by families with children attending the school. It makes economic sense for them to purchase a home for their child, allow him/her to bring along a couple of friends and live free, selling when they all graduate.

Parents not only don't pay for their child's accommodation (the friends pay the mortgage) but they usually realize a profit upon resale four to five years later. Sometimes these parents upgrade the home for personal reasons ("My son can't live in a dump!") and they are then more appealing as an investment later since they will attract better tenants and perhaps a higher rental rate. But these parents usually want a good return on their investment also. It's all relative in the end.

If you are going to do the renovation work yourself (often It's a matter of putting up a couple of walls, adding a bathroom, etc.) then you can turn a single family home into a student home relatively cheaply. If you are going to hire contractors, then your investment will have to be more long term in order to justify the initial outlay. Again, your real estate agent will likely know of a local contractor who specializes in student renovations (there are several in Hamilton). These contractors will build a safe environment but utilize cheaper materials. The students will appreciate the *new appearance* of the home but most are too inexperienced to realize that the materials used are of low quality. All renovations require permits from the City and can be obtained ahead of time with drawings. Of course, you have to ensure your plans adhere to the bylaws and inspectors will ensure that your renos are compliant with current building and fire codes.

Some investors choose to risk not obtaining permits and perform interior renovations without permission. No one suggests this is a wise thing to do, only that it is a common occurrence. The only time an inspector from the City will question what you are doing is if they are aware of it: if a neighbour complains about the noise; if a large construction bin shows up in the driveway; or if several construction vehicles surround the house. It is then pretty simple for compliance officers to notice your renovation.

It has become quite a cottage industry, therefore, for owners to quietly renovate basements without permits. When you go to sell your home, your real estate agent will insist on stating in the listing that the *seller does not warrant retrofitting or zoning allowances* or something similar in an effort to ensure that the next owner cannot come back to you if the City questions the renovations at a later date. It is very difficult for the City to charge an owner with renovating without a permit if there is no record of what the building looked like prior to your ownership which is why some investors take the chance. It should be noted, however, that although obtaining permits is time consuming and somewhat costly, most plans are approved (the City knows we need more student housing) as long as it complies with building and fire codes. Unfortunately, whether a renovated house has permits attached or not does not seem to affect the market value of the home. This is because compliance is not greatly enforced and homes often change hands several times before anyone in the City becomes aware that renovations have been completed. The market value of a student home is largely based upon the number of rooms for rent. Whether those rooms were permitted is not a major factor in establishing a selling price.

## Which is best?

Finally, the question of which type of home is the best for an investor. A lot depends upon your desire, skill and long-term goal. Turnkey homes are often kept for three to five years, then resold with a profit. Very little maintenance, upgrading, or renovating is achieved during the tenure and cash flow throughout the process has paid all expenses.

When renovating a home, you have to consider the additional expense of the renovations. If you spend $10,000-$30,000 on building additional rooms, upgrading kitchens and baths, etc., then it will be difficult to realize a return in five years just from rental income. However, the value of the home will increase dramatically, especially if you turned a three-bedroom family home into an eight-bedroom student residence. There are investors out there who are looking for freshly renovated homes capable of housing eight to ten students. Some investors *flip* such homes over a three to five-month period and realize a decent ROI upon resale. Others hang onto these homes for eight to ten years, ensuring a return on their reno investment during that time. Upon resale, their profit is substantial since cash flow over the tenure has already covered their renovation costs.

We should note also that due to the large number of the latter type of investors seeking properties, it is difficult to get a *bargain* on a home, even if it is in dire need of renovation. The potential returns are just so promising that often derelict homes will go into bidding wars, the winner being forced to pay several thousand over list price just to secure the property. Again, time will certainly allow this investor to recoup the additional costs, but it is not something for the weak hearted or inexperienced investor to contemplate.

Location is also a factor and something we get into later in this chapter. Homes closer to the school are usually more expensive than those farther away. Though this initially seems to be common sense, any real estate agent familiar with student housing will tell you that this is where the savvy investor can take advantage of the uninformed buyer.

For example, Homes south of Main Street, up to a mile away from the school, bring in the same monthly rents as homes a block away from the school. Why? Because homes farther away are newer, larger, and closer to amenities such as grocery shopping, bars, etc. Most students are not fazed by having to walk fifteen to twenty minutes if they can get a room that is larger, in a quieter neighbourhood, and is closer to grocery stores and bars. The pricing of homes for sale does not reflect this phenomenon and that is where a *bargain*, of sorts, can be had.

## Compliance and Licensing

Licensing student properties has always been on the table in all Cities across Canada and some have established bylaws enforcing landlords to obtain annual licenses in order to continue. Some of these programs have been successful, most have not. Licensing is little more than a method by which a City can garner a list of all available student properties with the initial intent of enforcing compliance to fire and building codes, as well as other related bylaws. In and of itself, this is not a bad idea. No good investor wants to be associated with slum lords and since student housing was initially the result of investors trying to make quick money off an unsuspecting tenant pool, it is forefront in the minds of those uninitiated in this type of investment. For the Cities who have approved finances it has become a cash cow. Thus the reason Hamilton City Council brings it up from time to time throughout the decades.

Students today are not as unsuspecting as in the past. Indeed, parents are much more involved when their young waifs leave home for the first time. Although not seeking luxury (in most cases), parents are demanding clean, safe, and monitored environments. The good investor provides these things.

Back to licensing. If the majority of the landlord base is willingly compliant to safety and cleanliness, what then is the use of licensing? Especially when, as in Hamilton's case, there are few officers employed by the City to actually ensure compliance throughout the area. The self-governing environment in Hamilton is one of the primary reasons licensing has never succeeded here.

Hamilton runs on a complaint-based system, meaning that unless someone--a neighbour, tenant, parent, etc.--complains about a problem with a property to the City, the home will likely never be visited. And even then, once a minor infraction is brought to the owner's attention, the majority willingly and quickly resolve the situation.

Seen by many as nothing more than a money grab by the municipality, it is arguable that licensing does nothing to improve student housing. And there are also the legal ramifications. Technically, there is no such thing as student housing as we've already mentioned. Investors are purchasing properties in areas of town zoned as single family housing. By assigning one lease to a group of students, they are in effect, complying to the law that a single family resides in the home. Should the City acknowledge that any particular home be licensed as a student home, then it can no longer be a single family residence. Would re-zoning be required? Or perhaps a new dwelling category would need to be established (something that has to be accomplished at a provincial or federal level).

In 2014, when the City of Hamilton brought the issue to a head and Council attempted to pass licensing of student rental properties, it didn't narrow its focus on student housing only but included all rentals (duplexes and triplexes included). That particular move was destined for failure. Both the local REALTOR® board and the Renter's Association formulated extensive research proving not only the destined failure of such a policy, but also its questionable legal validity.

The City promptly allowed the motion to drop and, for most people in the industry, licensing of any rental properties in Hamilton--student homes included--will not be brought up again for quite some time.

The only perceived negative to all of this is that when a particularly aggressive compliance officer or supervisor chooses to harass landlords, they are within their legal mandate to do so. If a deficiency is noted in a home, the Landlord could be charged with running an illegal lodging house. A court date would be set and a fine administered. In the two cases I know of where this has happened, the judge dismissed the cases once the landlords agreed to make the noted changes to their properties (which they had been willing to do prior anyway), and waived the fines.

The City must work with investors and everyone involved knows it. If anything, an aggressive stance by certain individuals within the municipal system is all that stops the cottage industry from running smoothly. Yes, there are still some slum lords around but with the pressure laid upon them by parents, students, the school, and even other investor neighbours, there is little need for the City to get involved. These landlords are slowly weeded out by the sheer power of economics. It is too easy to make good profit from student housing to allow a home to get run down so much that it can no longer compete in the marketplace. Sooner or later, that home is sold to a more responsible investor and a revitalized property is born.

As a result of all of the above, there is no list of student houses, nor the names of landlords in Hamilton. The closest thing would be to go to McMaster's Off-Campus Housing site, and look at all the properties listing rooms available to students.

# The Housing Zones

When a student decides to live in a student home rather than the limited accommodations provided by the school, they first choose an area they want to live in, and then begin a search within that area. Called *Zones*, each area, designated by McMaster and utilized by all rental companies, real estate brokerages, and the City itself, has unique features that attract certain types of tenants. Here are the zones as presented in the package given to new students from McMaster upon acceptance:

*https://macoffcampus.mcmaster.ca/ocrc_static/downloads/LivingOffCampus.pdf*

**Zone 1** (West Hamilton - both sides of Main St. W.) - Very high concentration of students.

Generally, a five to thirty-minute walk to campus. A highly residential area, there are many student homes

(three to eight bedrooms), basement apartments and high- and low-rise apartments located in these zones.

Close to grocery stores and pharmacies. Excellent bus service.

**Zone 2** (South West Hamilton/Downtown) and **Zone 3** (Hess Village/Downtown) – This area is a thirty to sixty-minute walk to campus. There are many high and low-rise apartment buildings, apartments in houses and duplexes for rent. Close to downtown shopping and excellent bus service.

**Zone 4** (Dundas) - Walking time to campus is fifty to sixty minutes. Small, quiet suburb of Hamilton bordering the north-west corner of campus. Some low-rise apartments, as well as rooms in residential
homes. Adequate bus service.

**Zone 5** (Ancaster) - A suburb of Hamilton. Very limited student accommodations. Some sabbatical listings available. Close to shopping and access to Highway 403. Limited bus service.

**Zone 6** (North East Hamilton) and **Zone 7** (South East Hamilton) - Varied rental accommodations available. Accessible by bus.

**Zone 8** (Hamilton Mountain) - Varied rental accommodations available. Accessible by bus, but requires transferring. More suitable for Mohawk College.

**Zone 9** (Outside Hamilton) - Varied accommodations in Burlington, Waterdown, Stoney Creek, Brantford, and other bordering cities/towns. Surprisingly adequate bus service between cities.

The majority of students opt to live in Zone 1 and it is a very large area surrounding the school. It is also the best area for investors but also the priciest. Proximity to the school is often considered important though I dispel that theory later on in the book. However, a lot of out-of-town investors simply look at a map and feel that anything outside of Zone 1--and even some on the outskirts of that zone--are too far away for any student to want to live. Despite being able to prove that theory incorrect, the majority of investors still prefer homes within a quarter mile of the school. As a result, these homes have greatly increased in value over the past ten years and, to many investors, don't make financial sense anymore. Homes to the south of Main Street (the street that runs directly in front of McMaster) average $100,000 lower in price than those on the north side. (Remember to check a map to understand that north actually faces the lake and south the escarpment). These homes are often newer, larger, and in better shape. They also command identical rents. Yet homes on the north side of Main St. continue to sell rapidly and for steadily increasing prices.

ZONE ONE includes the village of Westdale, a quaint community of shops, restaurants, coffee shops, banks, a theatre, and businesses. One of only two large grocery stores is on the outskirts of the village and is an easy walk for students on the east side of the school grounds.

Students who seek out this location enjoy a social life and interaction with the community. Residents tolerate, even encourage student housing as it lends itself to a vibrant existence. Several high-end restaurants have thrived here for years, despite the fact that the surrounding neighbourhood is approximately 80% student housing and none of those students can afford to eat there (unless Mom and Dad visit for the weekend). The coffee shops (at last count there were four) and quality fast food outlets thrive on the student population, as does the grocery store (a *No Frills®* at time of print). Small and large grocery outlets alike cater extensively to students providing inexpensive healthy foods as well as fast-food.

Zone 1 also includes Main Street which boasts several larger eateries including national chains. Most offer specialty menu items students can afford and some even provide entertainment throughout the week catered to the younger set. (Boston Pizza® on Main St. West has been running a Tuesday night University Trivia Night for several years.) The second grocery store (*Fortino's®* at time of print) is located on this strip but is a full service grocer catering to a higher density residential community nearby. Many of the businesses along the strip have a thriving residential customer base, drawing people from the village of Dundas, a community often referred to as the retirement capital of Southern Ontario.

The village of Westdale was once the upscale community reserved for executives of the steel industry. As such, many of the homes surrounding the village (especially near Churchill Park) are stately and large. Though many have been retro-fitted as student homes (with eight to ten rooms), many are still held by families who have lived there since its heyday as Hamilton's high-class enclave. Other larger homes nearer the campus were faculty properties owned by original administrators and professors at the university in the 1950s and 1960s. Those homes, though right next door to the school, rarely become student residences as they are traded to other faculty members at prices investors would never consider.

As Zone One slowly becomes more densely populated with student homes, there are few neighbourhoods left to explore as potential student neighbourhoods. Whitney (bordered by Hwy 2-Main St) and the Fortino's® store is the latest up-and-coming spot. Homes built in the 1950s and 60s are becoming available as the original owners are passing on. These are ideal student homes as they are usually three bedroom bungalows with large basement recreation rooms that can inexpensively become three to four rooms. Priced lower than other neighbourhoods in the zone, these homes boast seven to eight bedrooms with large common area living rooms, large back yards, and big rooms. Students who discover the neighbourhood always fall in love, despite it being a good half an hour walk to school. The (free to students) bus does pass along Whitney which would be a three to five-minute walk from any of these homes.

ZONE TWO, which is essentially the western end of downtown, consists of high-rise apartment buildings, residential homes with apartments or rooms available, and duplexes. More expensive than renting single rooms in a student house, these properties are not considered prime investment material.

In 2016, McMaster opened a downtown campus at the corner of Bay and Main Streets which houses a large number of medical and business students. A residence is part of the facility but there will be a need for accommodations in that area in the near future. Time will tell whether the immediate residential areas will experience the same reworking as a student mecca like Westdale since McMaster has carefully planned the facility to accommodate the majority of students. Since riding a bus in Hamilton is free to students, living in Zone 1 and taking public transportation to the downtown campus would not be difficult. Other smaller campuses have been in the downtown core for several years and some students have found accommodations in residential homes in the area. But it is not a prime investment center yet and may never be due to the stricter zoning laws and density of smaller single family residences.

All the other zones are too far away for most students to consider unless they have a vehicle or are willing to transfer buses several times. The exception is Zone 8 where there is an upswing in student residences close to the Mohawk College campus in the west end of the mountain. The area does not attract as many investors as West Hamilton because Mohawk is a community college and as such attracts local residents more than it does out-of-town students. The need for housing is not as great. Student homes in Zone 8 are less expensive than those in West Hamilton but keeping rooms constantly rented is a challenge. Most community college courses are shorter than their university counterparts and the turnover of tenants is much higher.

## Secondary Markets

In recent years, campuses outside of Hamilton (lumped together as Zone 9) have grown and there is an expanding population of students attending.

The Ron Joyce Centre in Burlington is home to the DeGroote School of Business MBA and executive education programs. Opened in 2010, it is a 90,000 sq. ft., building housing state-of-the art classrooms, meeting spaces and lecture facilities. It also provides executive education for the local business community in the Greater Toronto Area.

In 2013, McMaster and the Brant Community Healthcare System opened up a facility for residents and other health care learners at the Brantford General Hospital. The 10,000 sq. ft. space includes classrooms, offices, lounge spaces and *call rooms* or living spaces for residents on call. The facility is the new home for students of the Michael G. DeGroote School of Medicine and other McMaster healthcare students.

Brantford is slowly catching on in that it has already sanctioned one major private residence (the former Brantford Expositor building) and more will surely follow as the downtown core struggles to revitalize. Brantford is also home to the Law Campus of Waterloo University and the school busses students regularly from downtown to the campus.

There are also many older, single family homes close to designated campuses which are ideal for student housing. If the City learns from Hamilton and welcomes investors, then it could easily be the next student mecca for investors, fueled by up to three universities (McMaster, Waterloo, Wilfred Laurier).

Burlington is a little different. Currently, most of the students attending the Ron Joyce facility are bussed in from Hamilton where they reside. There is little effort in Burlington to accommodate students other than basement apartments in homes. City Council there is slow to recognize the growing population of students and bylaws are extremely restrictive. As land for the Ron Joyce facility was purchased through donations and fund-raising activities and built on prime business land, there is a possibility that when the need arises, additional land will be purchased to build accommodations for permanent students. Residential housing is set farther away from the campus and is not as conducive to a rental setup. McMaster has dedicated coaches travelling between the Hamilton and Burlington campuses.

A third emerging market nearby is St. Catharines, home of Brock University. As the university grows, adding more curriculums and therefore more students, the need for housing is growing exponentially. There were over 100 homes listed in the Brock Off-Campus Housing site at time of print and that is steadily expanding. We bring up this market because of pricing. Homes housing six to eight students are up to $200,000 cheaper than similar homes in Hamilton. Not yet as organized or as well known, Brock stands to be a good starting point for new investors. The school is located close to shopping and single family housing; there is little competition from apartment buildings, etc., and the school or city have yet to consider additional purpose-built facilities.

Burlington, Brantford and St. Catharines are all less than one hour away from Hamilton so out of town investors can consider multiple properties in these areas as personally manageable within a portfolio.

The final secondary market was mentioned earlier: Mohawk College. As with most community colleges, however, the student population is comprised mostly of local students. Many cities house community colleges and serve their communities and nearby ones with practical courses aimed at the needs of the community. As such, courses are shorter and students often find transportation to and from their family homes manageable. Pricing on the Hamilton Mountain--close to Mohawk College--is still lower than near McMaster. And there is an active Off-Campus Housing website run by the college. But most investors spend a great deal of time filling rooms on a regular basis. Larger homes with seven to eight bedrooms are almost always run partially empty as groups of students simply aren't in abundance at a community college. Smaller homes are easier to fill but pricing on the mountain has skyrocketed since 2010 and properties with only 4-6 rooms don't make financial sense anymore. The density of student homes to residences is also considerably lower and many neighbourhoods shun properties that are to be converted to student residences. Remember, Hamilton is a run on a complaint-based system, so if a neighbour chooses to complain about noise, over-population, garbage, etc., the City is more likely to force compliance to bylaws that are largely ignored in West Hamilton.

Student Housing

# Chapter Two:
# Financing

# The Parent as an Investor

The most unique type of investor is a parent, i.e.: a child has been accepted to a University far from home. The parent has two choices: get the child in residence, or find accommodations off campus. In most Canadian universities, getting into residence is difficult at best and even if you manage to win the accommodation lottery, most only allow a student to stay for first year. For future years, the student is expected to find alternate accommodations, thereby allowing new first year students access to the limited residences.

After initial research, a parent quickly realizes that the cost of accommodation is high. Single rooms can rent anywhere from \$350-\$600 per month... for a room. In their opinion, the homes are run by out-of-town landlords who do not take adequate care of the property and allow their precious children to live in what is, in their mind, one step up from the ghetto.

If that parent has any kind of investor savvy whatsoever, they quickly realize that they can purchase one of these homes, upgrade it to suit their standards, place their child in the master bedroom and rent out the remaining rooms to either their children's friends or other students.

Once their child graduates in four years or so, they put up the house for sale and use the proceeds to pay for the new graduate's first car, first apartment, etc., etc.

It doesn't take a math genius to realize that their child can essentially go to school for free. The down payment they need to purchase the house returns when they sell. Throughout the tenure of their child's studies, the other students in the house are paying the mortgage, expenses, upgrade costs, etc. and their child is getting free accommodation. Not only that but Mom and Dad can supervise the house and ensure there is no partying, no destroying of property, and no activity unbecoming of their offspring. They are usually surprised when, upon the sale of the house, they make a decent profit. In four years, their property has increased in value by at least $30-50,000 which more than pays for any upgrades they accomplished.

It is an experience they brag about to their friends and go to their graves thinking how clever they were to invest in their child's education.

In reality, it doesn't always work out that way but it happens often enough to ensure that the Parent Investor is a force to contend with in the student housing marketplace.
Parents are not always looking for the best value in a home and often pay high price for homes they deem appropriate for their children to live in. If they can't find such a home at the time, then they buy one that's close and upgrade it to look like the family home, where the child has been raised.
All this is well and good until it comes time to sell. A student home's real value is in the potential income it can generate, not necessarily its upgrades.

If a parent has spent thousands on a new kitchen, stainless steel appliances, upgraded bathrooms, new flooring, etc., that has little value to a regular investor who knows that most students couldn't care less about those things. Rooms rent for $450 in the Westdale/Ainslie area whether the kitchen has granite counters or if it still boasts the original orange Formica® So there is no value in the upgrades…

Unless you sell to another parent or an uninformed investor. You can always reduce the price to ensure a quick sale and still make a decent profit (since your main goal was to have your child live for free during his schooling), or you can hold out for an investor who feels the same way you do: namely that students are people too and should have the best accommodations available (those investors are out there but admittedly, the buying pool is shallow).

What the parent investor often does do is improve a derelict property, which is a good thing. Many investors will run a home for several years, enjoy the cash flow, and benefit from a tidy profit due to the fact they kept the property for more than five years, but without spending money on upgrades.

Also, as students move into second and third year, and get to know the area better, they realize that some homes are more modern and aesthetically pleasing than others, despite rent rates being essentially the same.

The majority of students are not heavily influenced by such things but that is slowly changing. For the investor that wants to keep the same tenants for their full four or five year terms, these types of amenities do attract a more discerning, responsible and appreciative tenant.

The only problem arises when the parent investor who has spent upwards of $50,000 in upgrades, believes his home should be valued that much more than homes that have not realized those upgrades. And that's where they're wrong. A regular investor may appreciate the upgrades, but he's not going to pay a premium for them. Not when he can get the identical house next door or down the street for $30-40,000 less without the upgrades. Most investors are willing to do some of the work themselves anyway and prefer to save money rather than pay for improvements that tenants may or may not appreciate.

And so, some parent investors leave town with a bad taste in their mouths. They improved the home for future students but no one recognizes those efforts. Tail between their legs, they go back home and eventually realize that since their child most likely just went through four years of university at no cost to them, maybe it wasn't a bad deal after all. All it required was a down payment. Overall, a good experience.

Oh, and on a final note. When we discuss financing later in this chapter, you'll see that when a parent purchases a student home it becomes merely a second home because a family member is living there. There is no need for a higher down payment (as required by a regular investor) and most banks will finance the property as they would any other rental investment. This distinction also carries other benefits including: the ability to remove current tenants (if you want to fill the house with your child's friends); the ability to finance and insure as a single family home; and the ability to renovate at will, to name just three. All of those above items become difficult when an investor is purchasing a student home with no family member in residence.

## The ROI-focused investor

Most investors are looking for a double digit return on investment (ROI) which gets harder and harder every year. For many Greater Toronto Area investors, many of the markets that used to be lucrative are now out of reach or no longer financially viable.

For the low-level investor ($100,000-$300,000), real estate for rentals simply doesn't exist anymore; especially in Toronto, Mississauga, Oakville and Burlington.
In Hamilton, rentable properties are still available for under the $400,000 mark, which is why the City is considered one of the best investment centers in the country. Single family, multi-residential and student homes are priced in the $250,000 - $500,000 range, though the latter is steadily increasing at a rate of about 15% per year. *(All figures are at time of print.)*

Double digit ROI's are difficult to obtain with purchase prices reaching the half a million-dollar mark, especially when most lenders demand a minimum 20% down. Who wants to tie up that much money on an ROI of 4-6%?

Which is why the informed investor looks at student housing. Purchase prices are high but income is high also, substantially higher than a regular rental unit. Whereas the average home in the Hamilton area rents for $1500-$2500 per month (the latter for high-end executive homes), the average student home rents for $2800-$3800 per month, depending upon how many rentable rooms there are.

When purchasing a single family home, especially a lower-priced one, an investor usually has to renovate flooring, kitchen, baths, add new appliances, etc., expending a fair amount of money upfront.

Students are not as demanding. Homes that haven't been renovated since the 1950's still sell for over $300,000, in their existing condition. With minor renovations (usually to add more bedrooms or showers), the home rents for upwards of $3,000 per month. The only caveat is that lenders are demanding higher down payments, anywhere from 25% -35% due to the unfair and out-of-date stigma attached to student housing (think the 1970's movie, *Animal House*)

Expenses in student housing are usually low also, and although the more successful student home landlords include utilities in rent fees, those fees are high enough to accommodate the expense. The only outrageous expense in student housing is internet. Students demand high-speed, high quality internet service and will put up with faulty plumbing, inadequate heating, outdated surroundings, and even messy co-tenants. But screw around with their ability to get online anytime and download anything... and you could have a mass tenant exodus on your hands.

With prices steadily increasing, even a student home that brings in $3500 a month may have a purchase price of $4-500,000. With 25% down.

# How homes are priced

To many investors, the pricing of student homes is a mystery.

What appears initially to be a lack of logic is easily explained when you understand the concept of student housing. Here are a few things to keep in mind about this type of property:

1)      Location has little impact on a student as no home in Zone 1 (the Westdale/Ainslie area) is more than a thirty-minute walk from McMaster. Most homes are on or near a bus route and city buses are free to students.

2)      First year students often search for homes alone but need parent approval before signing leases. After first year, the students are usually handling accommodations alone and have completely different search criteria.

3)      Students do not require much in the way of amenities. More than one shower is a must; bathtubs are not necessary (unless they are part of the shower); one kitchen is all that is required because most students don't cook (two kitchens are illegal anyway unless it's a full apartment on the second level). A microwave (or two) is essential.

4)      Arguably, common areas like a living room and dining room are unnecessary. Many investors convert these rooms into bedrooms. Groups of friends often seek common rooms and if you try to appeal to that market (earlier in the season), then it may be an advantage to have one. The common area is used for playing video games and partying, but that's also why many landlords eliminate common areas, opting instead for a nicely appointed kitchen, some with televisions, sans cable hook-up, mounted to a wall.

5)      Upgrades, other than additional showers, are usually wasted on students. They are looking for nice rooms to live in. If the kitchen has old appliances, linoleum flooring, and Formica® countertops, they aren't concerned. Spend your money on providing the best internet you can as that is THE most important feature for a student.

6)      Painting each bedroom at the beginning of each semester, and perhaps laying down cheap laminate flooring when carpets become threadbare, can go a long way towards making your home more rentable to students.

7)      Cost of rooms is vital. Students will pay the going rate but will always try to negotiate lower. Some will try to negotiate shorter leases (four to eight months), as they go home for the summer. The good investor ignores these requests and demands the signing of a twelve-month lease

at the going rate or higher. Out-of-town investors tend to allow negotiations simply because they fill their homes with the first students to approach them; they don't have the time to be discerning. However, acceptable rent rate ranges are clearly shown to each student in the package they receive from the school along with their acceptance letter. The good landlord does not stray far from this range.

8)      Students do not go to open houses, nor is there any logic to their search criteria. Students will call you to view available rooms 24/7, at their convenience, not yours. If you force it any other way, they will simply go to the next house on the list.


There are other things to consider, but those are the more important factors. What does this have to do with pricing?

Here comes the logic. A student house has value when it is fully leased for twelve months at the going rate or higher. If one or two rooms are empty, or if the leases are for eight months, the home is not as valuable because a new owner would have to fill those spots and missing months in order to be profitable. Trying to fill a student home mid-semester is virtually impossible as everyone has already found accommodations. Semesters start in May and Sept. Some shorter terms including international exchange students start in Dec and June but they don't account for much.

Students begin looking for May accommodations in January, especially groups of friends. By April, you will be renting single rooms, one at a time to the procrastinators or those who received their acceptance letters late.

Students looking for September accommodations begin around June. Groups of friends tend to start earlier. The risk of an eight-month lease is greater in September because most of these students go home the following May and don't want to pay for the summer months.

The best time to buy a student home is when it's full. Obviously, when you know what the income will be and what the expenses are, you can easily determine whether it's a good investment or not. The best time to find a full home is in May or September.

If you are looking at a home in any other month, you are going to carry the mortgage with whatever income it has at the time. If only 4 of 6 bedrooms are leased, you are not going to fill those other two rooms until a new semester starts. That difference in income is likely your profit.

Pricing of homes reflects this phenomenon, most of the time. Full homes with good leases are worth more than homes with some rooms empty. Of course, this has nothing to do with the house itself and that's what a lot of first-time investors misunderstand. If you're looking for a bargain, then a partially empty house may be the answer. Of course, you're going to carry it for a while until you can fill it again but maybe that works for you. Sometimes, a knowledgeable real estate agent will help you find a house anytime during the year, but negotiate closing either in April or July so that you aren't carrying it too long before the next semester. It is not that difficult to fill a home during those months.

Homes that have been upgraded don't always fetch a higher price. In fact, some investors resent paying a higher price for things they know have little value to students. Of course, derelict houses have the opposite effect but are almost always picked up by someone who feels they can renovate and make money. Usually, they spend too much on infrastructure issues which do nothing to add appeal to a student but are necessary.

It only works if they add multiple rooms and fill it with students. An empty house, any time of the year, has a lower value because most first-time investors are seeking turnkey operations as they find the process of finding students intimidating and time consuming initially.

Bidding wars are now the norm when it comes to student housing. There are so many investors out there, all seeking the same thing, that when a good house (meaning a full one within zone 1) becomes available, many investors are interested. Real Estate agents, of course, take advantage of the frenzy and disallow offers until a certain date, usually a week after listing the house. That way, several investors-especially out-of-towners-have the time to view the home and put together an offer. It is not unusual for a home to have 10-15 offers presented and the final price being $20,000-60,000 above list price.

Does that mean the investor paid too much?

It's all relative because when that investor decides to sell the home five years later, the same thing will happen. Student housing is a market niche that is growing at the same rate as the school's growth. McMaster is adding courses, facilities, and programming every year. Yet there are no new purpose-built accommodations (aside from the

Downtown campus). The City rejects many of the proposals and the risk for that type of investor is too high. The only such building, built on the old CNIB site, has been largely a failure due to high room costs. Parents love it, of course, because it's safe, environmentally friendly, and well administrated. But the students quickly learn that it's too expensive, too far away, and very restrictive... kind of like residence. After first year, most move out into a neighbourhood house, with friends. The school, of course, has little interest in providing additional residences due to cost and available land.

The uniformed investor will often offer below list price on a student home, only to be disappointed that a savvier investor takes it away in a bidding war. Student housing is not the place to practice those real estate strategies taught at seminars on "getting rich through real estate". Sellers rarely want to do a VTB (vendor take back mortgage) because they are trying to get their money out. They also know that their property is a hot commodity, and if handled properly, will sell for more than the list price.

**Who decides the list price?**

If the Seller is smart, he'll have the real estate agent do it. They know what similar houses have sold for in the area recently and will price it according to its value as a student house, not as a regular property. By pricing slightly below value, they can almost guarantee a bidding war, and therefore gain higher than list price, despite that price being considered fair value for the home.

If you are a parent investor, price will have little meaning other than what you can afford. But to the investor seeking a return, it is vital that the home has the future potential to be a money maker. Therefore, more rooms, larger rooms, and perhaps a common area and updated bathrooms is more important than a home close to the school, in better condition, but with fewer rooms.

Location is often misunderstood also. A lot of investors don't understand this which is why homes close to the school (King Newton, Arkell) often sell for higher prices than those on the south side of Main St. (Broadway, Emerson, Cline, etc.). When looking on a map, location is deceiving. Though homes on Arkell appear to be closer, homes on Broadway actually are closer. Arkell homes avg. $100,000 more than those on Broadway despite having the same number of rooms renting for the same prices. Homes in the Ainslie Woods area (south of Main) are newer than those in the Westdale Village area also, meaning rooms are larger and infrastructure (roof, furnace, plumbing, electric, etc.) are newer.

# Who is lending and what's the process?

Without a doubt, financing is the most difficult aspect of purchasing a student house. It is unlike any other property, even commercial, for two reasons:

1)     There is no such housing category--federally, provincially, or municipally--as student housing. Students live in either purpose-built facilities (residences), lodging homes, or single family residences (condos, apartments, and detached homes).

2)     Traditional banks maintain the stigma that student houses decrease in value over time due to the nature of the tenants. They are young people who are irresponsible, inexperienced or uncaring about home maintenance, are partiers, and live in groups of six or more, like a commune. Much of the stigma is based on American-style student housing like that portrayed in the 1970s movie, *Animal House*. Even in Canada, early student homes were not well maintained, often unsafe, and housed an unsafe number of tenants. Lenders feel homes depreciate faster under these forces.

Rather than apply a risk value to this type of housing, most traditional lenders simply say "no" to student house financing. Others make the Buyer jump through hoops, making it extremely difficult to qualify for a mortgage. Fifty-percent down payments, 100% security, etc., are just some of the demands thrown out.

The stigma is, of course, way out of whack. Yes, students have parties (mostly first-years) where they drink and smoke up. But this is by no means a regular occurrence. In fact, by second year, most students are so bogged down in studies (first-year failures having been weeded out), that what they really want is a quiet home with peaceful co-tenants. They are also getting more savvy in the art of leasing a room. Most will not stay in a home that houses more than eight people; many won't stay in a home that has a large common area (living room, sun room, etc.), because that's where they know parties will be hosted; and most now demand high maintenance and repair standards because they have been given copies of the Landlord/Tenant Act by the school and take the safety and cleanliness of their accommodations seriously.

Add to that the fact there are several hundred homes in the area, all competing for the same tenants and you have a phenomenon where landlords are outdoing themselves to attract students by improving their homes, ensuring safety, even *greenifying* them to encourage kids to sign on.

All of this is irrelevant because traditional banks simply aren't listening. The Royal Bank acquiesced in 2010 and came up with a package that focused on financing student homes, but with minimum 30% down payment. To those who have that kind of money floating around, here finally was one institution that recognized it was missing out on a booming business model.

The other major banks toy with the idea but want at least 20% down and secure assets. Most will not do it when approached directly. Some mortgage brokers have had success in dealing with Scotiabank and TD by playing liaison between a Buyer and the bank but it is still a long, drawn out process that often doesn't succeed.

One solution had been to not tell the lender that you were buying a student house. Unfortunately, this only leads to failure and sometimes loss of down payment. Banks always do appraisals on investment properties and when they get the report stating that the purchase is a student home, they pull the financing, sometimes just a week or so prior to closing-after you've already waived the financing clause in your Offer.

Some have better luck purchasing residences that have not been retrofitted as student homes yet. In this manner, the bank feels it's financing a regular single or double family residence. Once the deal closes, the Buyer begins renovations and no one's the wiser. until it comes time to renew the mortgage and then the above scenario takes place and the mortgage is refused.

Some have tried the commercial route. Interest rates are higher, as are down payments, but by showing the value of the leases in place, the commercial lender looks at returns rather than value of the property. Unfortunately, most of the deals done this way don't make financial sense when rates are so high.

The most successful route is to use a mortgage broker who has done a student deal before and who works with second tier lenders. Trust companies and places such as National Bank or Laurentian Bank have been known to perform student home mortgages. Their down payment demands are similar to traditional banks but they seem to understand the product better (many such banks have branches in student centers) and recognize the niche first tier banks are ignoring.

Lastly, third tier lenders such as trust fund groups, investor groups, etc. will welcome a proposal for a student home. Usually they are looking for more than one investor who is going to purchase more than one home, thereby forming more of a property management company. Their rates are higher than second tier but lower than commercial so sometimes it's a fit. The key is finding a mortgage broker who has access to those types of funds.

**The process**

When you've found the house you want to purchase, ideally you want to include a finance clause allowing you up to ten days to obtain a mortgage. Most real estate agents specializing in this market know that it takes longer to confirm a student house mortgage than any other type and will allow this. (The normal finance clause is 5-7 days). It doesn't seem to help even if you have a pre-approval ahead of time. Every student home is treated differently. In addition, if a home has been flagged by the banks, meaning it is known to be a home that is traded often, needing repair, has more than eight rooms, or any other related stigma, the head office may override the local lender and pull financing. This information is readily available to them through their access to the MLS® system.

If your agent knows what they're doing, they will also ask the selling agent to remove any content in the MLS® listing that mentions students, proximity to McMaster, etc., after your Offer has been accepted, as this reduces the risk of a bank refusing to finance. Keep in mind, however, that the majority of agents do not perform their own paperwork at that level and do not have the ability to alter MLS® listings at will.

The next step is the inspection. Most student homes are not up to the standards of even a low-income residence. But you're not looking for that type of residence. You want a safe house, a house where all infrastructure components have been addressed (furnace, roof, windows) and a house which has sufficient bathrooms for the number of tenants. Aesthetics are not important. Paint, new drywall, upgrading kitchens, etc. can all be done later. You want your inspector to focus on plumbing, electrical, water damage or the potential for it--especially in basement areas--and, most importantly safety code. Remember, there is no such category as student housing so your inspector can't tell you everything's legal. Often, the lower level rooms are not up to building code and this is a risk inherent in student housing (we discuss that more later). What you're looking for is safety and size. Can a student safely and comfortably live in this environment? Of course, simple safety rules such as every bedroom having an egress window (a window large enough for a tenant to climb out of in case of fire) are essential. A bedroom without a window is clearly unsafe and definitely wouldn't pass any compliance inspection. On the bright side, windows can now be put into the side of homes for under $400 so it's not a major issue, just one you need to be aware of.

Once you have done everything the bank asks of you-- providing all the documentation they require--you will get the go-ahead to remove the condition. If the house passed inspection--or at least if you and your agent negotiated with the Seller to a level, you are both comfortable with--then the house is sold. If the closing date is nearby, your lender will send out an appraiser and as long as the home is exactly what you said it was, the financing will go through. One hint here is to remove all locks on individual rooms. It is illegal to have a room locked despite the fact that every student house does it. Students demand locked rooms, the school indirectly supports the act, and parents insist. But the banks don't want it because it's against fire code. Simply take off all the handles prior to the appraisal and put them on again afterwards. Insane, I realize, but it has saved many a mortgage from being pulled in the past. The lenders use local appraisers and every one of them in Hamilton is aware of student housing. They won't lie and you can't get them to ignore things. If there are no locks on the door, they won't report it. What you are doing is clear to the appraiser but he only reports what he sees, not what he doesn't see; a fine line I agree, but one that has worked to date.)

If the closing date is a few months away (often negotiated when you buy a house part way through a semester) then remember the home won't be appraised till near the date of closing. Your financing isn't really secure until that appraisal is completed and the lender is satisfied. That's why it's important to be very upfront about what you're buying. I have met investors who say "I have a great relationship with my bank. I've got several properties already. They'll do it and for 10% down too."

When I hear statements like that, I drop the client. They are uninformed and will not succeed. If you are selling your student home, be sure you know that the person buying it isn't such an investor because you are all wasting your time. I have not seen a lender finance a student home for less than 20% in the past ten years… for anyone.

Finally, whatever deal you make to mortgage your new student home today, things will be different when you renew. Re-financing is the norm, once you're established. Many investors use the equity built up in their first student home to purchase a second one. The original lenders are much more apt to do so when you've proven yourself. This is why many investors struggle to get a student home initially, only to move on to own three or four within five years or so. Financing is much simpler the second time around.

## Down payment and Deposit

### Down payment

We have briefly touched on this but it should be made clear.

No matter how good a relationship you have with your bank, no matter how many properties you and your neighbourhood lender have purchased together, and no matter how much you think you know about real estate investment strategy...

Unless you've bought a student house before, you're in for a surprise. If your friendly banker hasn't done one either, he'll initially have positive feedback for you. But once his supervisor or head office catch wind of it, they'll insist he refuse the mortgage. There is no sound reason for this other than what has been explained before: the stigma of student housing being a negative investment; and the fact that any lawyer will advise against it because it an uncategorized (in other words illegal in his mind) housing category.

There is no use trying to explain the merits of the investment; even if your personal lender likes the idea, someone higher up--at least in the traditional banks--will kybosh it relatively quickly. If you waste time trying to convince them, you'll use up your conditional sale period and lose the house you're trying to buy.

Mortgage brokers are more apt to welcome your business but the majority of them will shy away from student housing for similar reasons. But if you find a broker who has done it successfully before, it will be a marriage made in heaven. They'll know what you need to do, what your agent needs to do, and who to take the proposal to. More often than not it's a second tier lender or trust company that recognizes the niche. Many a second tier bank has garnered new clients simply by being more accessible to less-than-perfect investment proposals.

Regardless of who lends you the money, however, they will want a minimum 20% down. Even if you've bought investment properties for lower, you'll find no one will touch a student house without 20% minimum. Many-even second tier lenders-require 30%.

I will even be as bold to suggest that if your lender proposes doing a mortgage for less than 20%, you very seriously question whether it will go through after the appraisal. Remember, many student homes sell for the prices they do because of their income or income potential. But that isn't taken into account on a standard appraisal; all the appraiser is doing is setting a value for the house as a single family residence. Often, the two numbers are several thousand dollars out of whack. When that happens, the lender will ask you to make up the difference.

For example, let's say you purchased an eight-bedroom student house for $400,000. You know it's worth that because you won it in a bidding war, so everyone else thinks so too. But as a single family home it is only a four-bedroom (extra basement rooms don't count in single family), and it is appraised for $370 by the bank. You've already put 20% down but now the bank wants you to make up the difference between what it feels the house is worth ($370) and what you paid ($400). So you have to come up with another $30,000, and most likely you find this out a week before closing because that's usually when the lenders do appraisals. You can't make an appraisal a condition of your deal most of the time because the banks simply won't do it fast enough and no seller will wait when there are others ready to buy.

As mentioned before, when you purchase your second student home, you will likely be able to use the equity you've made on the first one to finance the down payment. But if it's your first student home be ready for anything. Some of my clients have paid up to 45% down in order to get a home financed at the last minute. Most would have walked away had they known they would have to tie up that much funds.

## Deposit

Most investors know the difference between a deposit and a down payment but just in case, let's clarify because it is different with student homes.

A down payment is the percentage of the home's purchase price that the lender expects you to provide, without financing. So, if your home is $400,000, and they require 20% down, you need to have $80,000 available. You'll also need closing cost of around $3-5,000 separate to this so the bank knows you can close (lawyer fees, mortgage fees, etc.).

But when you make an offer on a home, you need a deposit--within 24 hours of making that offer--to give to the selling real estate brokerage. They do not hold the cheque, they cash it and hold the funds in trust against commissions. That money is part of your $80,000 down payment but you need to have it ready the day you buy.

Here's the kicker. Because student housing is considered an investment by all involved, the deposit requirements are higher than with single family homes. Deposits average from $10,000 to $30,000 depending on the brokerage, the seller, and the house itself. If the house is popular and likely to go into a bidding war, the seller wants to know you are serious so that he doesn't make a mistake with taking a chance on choosing your offer. If you are willing to part with $10,000 to secure the deal, that's a pretty positive sign you mean business. In addition, many buying agents use the deposit to garner favour with selling agents by showing their client is more serious than others by putting up higher than requested deposits, like $25,000 or $30,000. The concept is redundant really because it's all part of the down payment anyway so it's not like the buyer is paying more. But he is putting out more of his down payment earlier, telling a seller he has plenty of available funds and won't be a financing risk.

Why is this important?

Because more student house deals are lost due to lenders not approving financing than any other reason. If you want to ensure your financing won't be an issue, be sure you have your mortgage broker or bank lined up ready to move as quickly as possible. They'll still want five days or so but at least you will have provided most of the personal paperwork they needed ahead of time. Then all they have to deal with is the house itself. Condition periods (the time between making an offer and waiving all your conditions such as financing and inspection), are no time to be providing income statements and asset lists to your lender; that should have been done ahead of time.

Many investors use their line of credit for deposits, then either repay it prior to closing, or convince the lender they can carry both the investment and the line of credit. If the LOC has been established for a long period, the odds are it will be allowed. Funds from other sources like RSP's, Tax accounts, etc., may be usable but your financial advisor will have to explain the benefits or drawbacks of using those avenues.

# Making an Offer

We need to discuss this process, even if you've done it many times before, because with student housing the likelihood of you being caught up in a bidding war is very high. And bidding wars are a very different breed.

When a house is priced at market value or slightly higher, the seller anticipates negotiation. On average, $5,000-$10,000 reduction of list price, tends to be the norm. In a Sellers' market (where there is not much inventory and a lot of Buyers), that number diminishes greatly. And in a Buyers' market when there are a lot of properties for sale but fewer buyers looking in that price range, then the price can sometimes go lower.

Not so in student housing. The house is worth what it's potential income is worth. Having said that, some homes that are in perceived great locations, or have been improved dramatically, will fetch higher than their income potential suggests. (Remember, perceived great locations aren't necessarily accurate and the savvy investor will usually ignore that when it comes to proximity to school.)

Regardless, if the home is fully leased with a minimum of seven bedrooms, you will find that many investors are interested. If the Seller's agent knows what he's doing, he will force a bidding war by not allowing offers for several days after initial listing. This allows all buyers--including out-of-town investors--the opportunity to view the home at their convenience. The frenzy this often creates is physical as well as psychological. Usually, the waiting period is over the weekend and every interested investor shows up during that two-day period, making the property look even hotter. Offers are usually registered by email (as no agent wants to compete in person at the Seller's home or the agent's office along with several other agents) and they are considered, in the order they arrive, and decided upon.

In days gone by, bidding wars were not as frequent and logic prevailed. Then suddenly, once a lot of investors realized the value of student housing, bidding wars were occurring on every house that qualified. If fifteen offers arrived, that meant fourteen buyers went away disappointed. If you didn't want to be one of those fourteen, then you made sure your offer was as good as it could be.

Often, that meant offering well over asking price, hoping to outbid others who were equally interested. In 2016, I attended four such bidding wars in the month of March and every one of them took the selling price to more than $40,000 over list price. Who can guess what the price is going to be?

Actually, now that this phenomenon has been going on for a while, there is a formula that seems to work fairly well and is agreed upon by several real estate agents working in this field.

Every condition (finance, inspection, lawyer approval, etc.) is worth apx. $5,000 to a Seller. And every registered offer will raise the price by apx. $5,000 also. Therefore, if a house is listed for $399 and has ten offers, this formula would tell you that you need to offer minimum $450 to obtain that property.

Sound silly?

It's proven to be a valid benchmark. But only if the property qualifies. If the home needs a lot of work to bring it up to even student standards, but is in a prime location, you'll still get the bidding war, but the price per offer will be closer to $3,000, meaning that above mentioned home would sell for $430 or so.

Why are conditions worth so much?
As mentioned before, more student home purchases fail due to financing than any other factor. If your offer eliminates the financing condition, not only have you increased your offer by apx. $5,000 in the seller and selling agent's mind, but you have assured them that financing is not going to be a problem.

The second most important factor that causes failure in purchasing is inspection. Many student homes have not been well maintained. Some could use upgrades, repairs, or improvements. Often, after an inspection reveals multiple glaring issues, a buyer will want to renegotiate the price to accommodate some of the work. So, when making an offer, if you eliminating the inspection clause you're telling the seller that this will not happen. Again, that's worth about $5,000 in the agent's mind.

If any offer has one of these conditions, the seller runs the risk that either financing won't be approved or the house will not pass inspection. Either of these means the house is back on the market. Will the other buyers who entered the bidding war come back? Not always. Often, there are equally good houses in the neighbourhood and the same group of buyers simply shift their attention to the next one. Even if you get one of them back, they are no longer in a bidding war situation, so they are not going to offer even list price. More likely, they'll go lower, knowing that your property has lost its momentum and you may never see multiple offers again.

The reality, therefore, is that if you want to win a bidding war on a student house--a property that has no emotional attachment to the buyers bidding--then you need to be well over list price, and remove all conditions, meaning it's a firm sale the second the seller signs the Offer.

Such strategy separates the men from the boys, so to speak. Only those who are secure in their financing, are not worried about repairs or upgrades, and are educated enough to know when a price is too high, will survive in this environment.

# Chapter Three:
# The Tenant

# First Year vs. Post Grad

Choosing the right tenant for your student home is critical to its success. And it's mostly common sense.

Students who have just received their acceptance to first year university are, of course, searching for accommodation immediately. Some years, however, those letters don't go out from the school until well into the summer (July, August).

But you want to know your home is rented sooner than that (May, June). Second, third, fourth, and post-grads are already in town and are looking for homes much sooner- especially if they've tried it before and have come to realize that if they don't start early, the pickin's are slim.

The advantage to first-year students is that parents are usually involved. That means they come with their child to view homes (making the showings more reliable) and they often don't want to waste several weekends doing so, and therefore make decisions quickly. They are looking for clean, organized homes that are close to the school and operated by someone who pays attention to the property (in other words, a local or management company). Parents are also usually paying the bills the first year so you don't have to worry about bouncing cheques, etc. Even if the new student is paying, it is usually a simple matter to ask the parents to sign the lease as a guarantor. They are very involved with their child's life at this point. By second or third year, that involvement drops off dramatically, regardless of how *close* the family is. University students develop independence very quickly.

Which brings us to another point. First year university is primarily a *review* year: what my university son likes to call a breeze through. It's not that difficult. Therefore, first year students have a lot of free time. And since this is often the first time away from home for an extended period, they want to expand their wings.

Which means they party a lot. If you've rented your home to a bunch of first year students who are friends, you are assured payment will be on time and accurate. You can also be assured your house will be treated like a scene from *Animal House* by the end of the first term.

Of course, this is a generalization and there are some kids who are very studious, very subdued, and, therefore, very good tenants. Mom and Dad either come to visit every weekend, or the kids go home. Either way, the home doesn't suffer from any pernicious and destructive attitudes.

# What are the Students looking for?

Although we touched on this in the last section, understanding what students are looking for in accommodation will help you understand what your home should and should not provide.

First year students who show up with Mom and Dad are looking for homes that resemble their own homes. This is totally unrealistic, of course, and after they've viewed a few their expectations drop dramatically.

A student residence should be safe and reasonably clean. I say reasonably because you must remember you are dealing with a group of young people who are most likely experiencing their first venture away from home, may or may not know their co-tenants, and are used to having Mom clean, cook, wash dishes, and wash clothes... usually (no stereotype intended but I've been proven right too many times to ignore the fact).

In later years, when Mom and Dad aren't as involved, the students are still looking for clean and safe, but they now usually also want quiet space with a landlord that fixes things and deals with complaints quickly and effectively.

## Distance

Is distance from the school a factor? Definitely with first year students who are influenced by their parents. But for everyone else, not really. Due to the landlocked nature of the neighbourhoods surrounding McMaster, no house is more than a thirty-minute walk from school. Bus service goes virtually everywhere (save for a few blocks close to the escarpment) and is free to students.

The school will tell you there are several zones of student housing but in reality there is only one: Zone 1. The boundary extends from the school west to Hwy 2 (the edge of the village of Dundas), north to the Lake, south to the escarpment, and west to the 403. This is where 95% of all students reside.

With the addition of a downtown campus in 2016, there are residences on the other side of the 403, closer to downtown, but that is an emerging market that is still an unknown from an investment perspective. The City allowed Macmaster to build residences on campus so there is debate about how much off-campus housing will be required. If time reveals that housing will be needed, then the North End of Hamilton may see some increase in investor interest. However, as prices are already high in that area, and since most homes would require retro-fitting to accommodate multiple students, the ROI will likely not be as strong as that of homes in Zone 1.

**Price**

In years gone by, the price of rooms was directly related to: 1) distance from school; 2) size of rooms and number of rooms in the house; 3) number of bathrooms and kitchens; 4) condition of the home.

These days, however, #2 and 4 are the predominant factors that determine price. Kids don't really need a lot of space outside their rooms (i.e.: living room, eat in kitchen, dining room, rec room, etc.). What they want is privacy and enough space for a bed, desk, dresser, large screen TV (for video games) … and that's about it. When they do congregate, it's usually in a bedroom, not a common area. Most students have their own TVs and computers which is why student residences rarely offer cable service. (Personal TVs are predominantly for video gaming)

Access to a clean, decent washroom would come next. A spacious kitchen, for the most part, is not vital as most students either use a microwave oven exclusively, or eat out. Certain nationalities seek full-size kitchens (international students especially), but unless you cater to that class of student, it is not very important. (Keep in mind that parents think it's essential, despite many knowing their children couldn't cook if their lives depended upon it.)

Distance is no longer a factor simply because price has caught up with sanity. The school suggests (in their welcome package to students) that they pay around the $450 mark all included (at time of print). Lofts, rooms with ensuites, and retro-fitted master suites will go for more, and basement rooms will go for less, but the average is around that figure.

When prices exceed this amount (as they have in other University towns), investment lags and those Cities are forced to re-assess their attitude toward student housing. They invite offshore money and hungry developers in, and next thing you know the town is inundated with purpose-built student housing--mega-apartment buildings, and no one is happy. Just ask the students in Waterloo and Toronto. No one wants to pay $600 a month for a tiny room shared with two or three others, despite having a nice kitchen and bath. With up to 30 kids per floor (in some instances), these buildings quickly become what I call *academic slums*. Although well-maintained, they are basic, utilitarian, and un-appealing to most students. (One such project was hatched in Hamilton in the former CNIB institute building on Main St. and despite the City deeming it a success, those of us in the business know that the turnover is extremely high, as is the cost of each unit. The building is at the very edge of Zone 1, requiring bus transportation, and most of the rooms are occupied by first-year students. For obvious reasons, parents love it: It's safe, all-inclusive and self-contained, and it resembles residence. After one year of this, most of the kids opt out to live elsewhere within Zone 1 in a four to nine-bedroom student residential home.

## Location

There are only two grocery stores within Zone 1 and neither are ideally located. FreshCo took over the site at Longwood and King St. (the outer edge of Zone 1) late in 2015; and Fortino's is situated below Main St., halfway into the Zone coverage area. The village of Westdale offers variety stores, restaurants, a couple of bars, coffee shops, etc., and provides the quintessential village atmosphere. Kids either love it or hate it and choose accommodations accordingly. Westdale is at the eastern end of Zone 1 and if you look on a map, appears to be close to campus. However, if you're an engineering student, you're adding another half mile to your walk as the main building for Engineering is on the western side of campus. In fact, after first year, kids will choose accommodation based on the side of campus most of their classes are on. For example, Engineering is on the West side, Medical and Business on the East. Athletics, etc. are at the back/middle, and the Children's Hospital is at the front facing Main St. There are homes within 500 yards of each of these facilities and you'll find that students congregate in similar neighbourhoods close to their classrooms and study halls.

If a student can pay $450 to live on King St. just down from campus, or the same amount for a room on Broadway, down near the escarpment, why would he/she choose the latter?

Primarily, homes on the south side of Main St. are larger and newer. The neighbourhood was built in the 1950s and 1960s mostly, whereas homes closer to Westdale Village were built in the 1920s and 1930s, some even earlier. Rooms in the homes to the south of Main St. are usually in bungalows and tend to be larger and are located on either a main or lower level floor. The older homes in Westdale are often two or three-storey homes with low-ceilinged basement levels.

There aren't really any amenities south of Main St (other than the restaurants and bars on Main St. itself), so the neighbourhoods are quieter, lots are larger, and there is usually more parking (though that isn't a major concern for struggling students).

## Density

Over the past ten years, the density of student housing in the Westdale/Ainslie Woods communities has increased dramatically. Although there is no *official* designation, those of us REALTORS® buying and selling homes regularly in the area know that it is close to 80% at time of print. There is a gathering of high-end residential homes north of Westdale (close to Princess Point and the Lake) but each time one goes up for sale, it is quickly lapped up by an investor (inevitably in a bidding war) and retro-fitted to become a multi-room residence for students. In 2012, I sold a well-known tenured music professor's home just five doors down from campus. He insisted we not turn it into student housing but the Buyer convinced him he would retain the character of the early-century home. That home is now a 9-bedroom residence with a gourmet eat-in kitchen, gumwood doors with glass plating, complete with huge picture window overlooking an expansive rear yard.

Eventually, all the homes in the area will be student residences. We know this because City Council currently insists that no multi-level homes/apartments will be built within Zone 1. In fact, the *monster clause*--a bylaw restricting new and reno'd building height and size--has been in place since 1997. You can see the result of this sudden and impactful bylaw when driving along Ward or Royal Avenues where 10-bedroom homes have been erected beside 2-bedroom cottages. Prior to the bylaw, anything was possible. Not anymore, though some believe that may change as accommodation needs become more dire in years to come.

Of course, this is why existing student homes-or the remaining residential homes available-are so valuable. Investors must maximize those homes to accommodate as many tenants as possible because renovating to create a larger home is a very difficult, expensive task (though not impossible-see Chapter Five).

The kids don't care about density within Zone 1. In fact, they welcome streets that are 100% student residences as they feel safer and more involved in a community of sorts. There are also fewer families on the street to complain about noise, excessive garbage, etc.

Density within each home is more critical. Once they pass the first-year *weeding-out of also-rans,* most students understand that privacy is tantamount to their success. Partying is a thing of the past (or at least restricted to after-exam gatherings in April and August). So many of them are attracted to smaller homes; homes with 4-6 rooms, as opposed to homes with 8-10 rooms. This creates a dilemma for the investor because a home with only 6 rooms that costs over half a million dollars simply doesn't make sense. And although maximizing space is vital, many homes can't accommodate an expansion to more than five rooms simply due to their design. Many older students seek these smaller homes out and once rents match investment, they may become viable again for an investor. At the moment, however, most of the smaller homes are purchased by parents seeking accommodation for their own children.

## Lease length

Ask a student and they'll say they only want to rent during semester which is either Sept to May, or May to May with the summer months off. Some students attend for only four months and only want to sign leases for that period.

You are an investor and you need income twelve months of the year. Most students, parents and academic personnel understand this. But many still try to make things work for them. Smart landlords insist on a twelve-month lease, allowing the students to try and sublet for the summer months when they aren't there. But uneducated landlords will allow the eight-month lease (Sept-May), let them go home for the summer, and return for a new lease the following September. Those are the landlords that have a hard time making money.

As an investor, you should insist on a twelve-month lease and have parents sign as guarantors in case the student reneges during the summer. You'll always have students who will sign the lease but disappear anyway, and it's up to you whether you chase them or not. Personally, I find it cheaper and less of a headache to simply find another tenant. Not everyone agrees. If you can get a parent to sign as guarantor, great, but many refuse. And the few times I've heard of a landlord taking a tenant to court, the cost of the case far exceeds any funds they have received from the delinquent tenant. Again, it's easier, quicker, and less painful to simply find someone else. Even if the room is empty for three or four months, you'll find it's cheaper than hiring a lawyer. If you're lucky enough to get a delinquent tenant to show up for a tribunal hearing, you may avoid legal costs, but the odds are definitely against you.

## Laundry

A contentious issue for some. Most investors believe you should provide a washer and dryer for tenants to use free of charge. Some landlords purchase expensive coin-operated units that force students to pay for laundry and the negative attitude it creates within the household virtually guarantees those tenants will move out when the lease is up. There are simply too many landlords providing appliances free of charge and in good working order.

## Utilities

I have found it far easier to rent a room when all utilities are included. When a student who has likely never been responsible for rent before comes up against an unknown (what utilities will cost), they shy away from it. They prefer to know what things will cost. By simply increasing the rent you want by the amount you feel each room should cost you, you'll find it much easier to rent the rooms. Put the utilities in your name (so the hydro company won't shut electricity off when a bill isn't paid by tenants) and simply divide the costs by the number of rooms. On average, utilities cost $40 per room, per month (at time of print). If yours are higher, check how warm they keep the house. Many international students are shocked by Canadian temperatures during the winter and keep thermostats high. Internet will be the most expensive utility but it is also the most important. Cogeco and Bell both have great plans for student houses.

# Who's paying?

For first year students, Mom and Dad are usually footing the bill. They have not only paid thousands of dollars for tuition, but are also prepared to pay for accommodation. They understand that student housing is a necessity and although some will try to negotiate an eight-month lease, most don't push it and will ultimately sign a 12-month lease. And they will sign on as guarantors also, especially if you don't give them a choice.

Remember, in most cases, this is usually the first time their child has left the security of the family home and the parents are invested in ensuring the experience of security and safety for their child. This results in a willingness to accept full responsibility for their child's actions, at least for the first year. You'll be paid on time and in full. But you'll have to put up with their inane demands such as: "Can we put security bars on the windows?"; "Can we not have a full kitchen complete with dishwasher?"; or my favourite: "Is there a maid service?". How you respond is entirely up to you but suffice to say that your only legal responsibility is only to provide a safe, clean environment.

For many landlords, the assurance of payment outweighs the headaches of dealing more with Mom and Dad than the tenants themselves.

But for others, second-year to post-grads are the preferred tenant. Mostly because Mom and Dad have mysteriously disappeared from the equation. After first year, regardless of the relationship between parent and child, you'll see a drop in communications between child, parent, and you. Once the novelty wears off, the kids are left alone to make decisions.

Many get jobs in the area-at restaurants, grocery stores, variety stores, or McMaster itself. Mom and Dad quickly realize that the kid is growing up and should be, at least partially, supporting him or herself. And once that happens, the purse strings are severed, albeit sometimes with very dull scissors, and the student fends more from themselves. That doesn't mean Mom and Dad aren't involved anymore, it just means they aren't making *all* the decisions. Including where the child lives... and how much they will pay.

## OSAP

As tuition costs skyrocket, and single-parent families become more common, you'll often come across a student who is financing his tenure at University via OSAP (Ontario Student Assistance Program). This is a government program where Ontario actually subsidizes kids who come from lower-income environments and, in effect, lends them the money to attend university. (Other provinces have similar programs). When you consider that recent changes to OSAP allow for the recipients to pay no more than $7000 per year back to the government (regardless of what tuition costs), there is an increase in kids attempting to qualify. In situations where parents are divorced, it is relatively simple for a student to use the lowest income parent as guarantor, ensuring that they receive the largest amount allowed each year.

What this means is that the student must wait until the government puts the borrowed money in their account. And as you might expect, the government is often late. The first one or two month's rent may be late and if your tenant tells you it's because of OSAP, you'll have to trust them (unless the parents guaranteed). Once the student receives their funding, they can of course catch up immediately. OSAP funding is split in half for those attending full semesters; one in September and the second in January.

## Freedom

For those who find themselves suddenly in charge of their own finances, the experience is both overwhelming and enlightening. They suddenly realize that if they can reduce costs in one area (rent), they can have more available/disposable income for other things (partying, eating out, dating, video game). The first item to hit the chopping block is rent. The less adroit kids will start to be late paying rent (because they went out to restaurants too much last month and need to wait for the next paycheque), and the more aggressive will attempt to break their lease and find somewhere cheaper (a process worthy of a chapter in itself).

Ultimately, you as a landlord, must ensure that your tenants pay on time (within 3 days of the first of the month is the acceptable norm), and that they share in responsibilities of keeping the house in good running order (take out garbage, wash dishes, clean the tub, etc.). This is, of course, as much an art as it is a science. Kids will tell you they'll participate in chores but will then forget, angering both you and other tenants. You will have to deal with this. Notices on the fridge, etc. usually instigates action but sometimes doesn't. At this point, you have a decision to make: either enforce it with your presence, hire a maid to come in regularly, or suck it up and do it yourself. As for rent, if a tenant forgets, then constant reminders are necessary. If they are waiting for a paycheque, you essentially have to wait. There is a section later on evicting tenants. If you're having trouble getting rents on time, read it. The rules protect the tenant more than the landlord and although that may not seem fair to you, it's the law.

# What to expect from your tenant

As previously mentioned, your can fully expect to be paid rent but not necessarily on time, of course. The rights of the tenant allow for a lot of leeway here. Even if you begin the process to evict your tenant (which can take up to 90 days), if they choose to catch up with rent within that period, your eviction paperwork becomes null and void.

You can expect them to be tardy in cleanliness and related chores. Students away from home for the first time often assume you will do the garbage, mop the floor, change light bulbs, even do the dishes. Unless you specify--in writing and posted where they can easily see it--that they are responsible for all duties involving the upkeep of the house, they won't do it. They will sometimes complain that their studies make it too difficult. They will try to blame one of the other tenants ("It's Dave's turn for garbage this week, not mine"). They will simply ignore the chores to the point where you will need to hire a truck to clear out the debris in the backyard. It is not uncommon for the tenants to throw garbage bags in the back yard, forget to put them out on garbage day (and in Hamilton you can only put out one bin of regular garbage), and not notice when racoons suddenly see your house as the latest free buffet centre.

If you are an out-of-town owner, the accumulation of garbage and dishes, etc. will creep up on you if you're not regularly visiting and reminding tenants of their obligations. This is when you decide whether you need a property manager. There are two or three good ones in Hamilton and they aren't overly expensive. Drop me an email (at back of book) if you want their contact info.

One alternative is to reduce the rent of one of your more responsible students and make them house manager. They either do all the duties themselves or create a list whereby all tenants participate. They are responsible for the success of this mission, or their rent goes back to normal. Picking the right tenant can be a challenge. Everyone's up for a rent reduction. But they don't really think you're serious about them playing house Mom.

When the semester is coming to a close and exams are over, this is the danger period. The kids feel great relief and like celebrating... meaning party. If they are going home at the end of the semester, the results of the party may well be left for you to deal with (i.e.: empty beer bottles, leftover pizza, mysterious plastic red cups everywhere, and maybe even a couple of fist-sized holes in the drywall). If your house has a large common area like a living room, you are more susceptible to the partying. Homes without the room simply don't attract partying, another good reason to make that living room another bedroom. (Lots of homes utilize the kitchen as the only common area in the home).

Clean up after semester includes removing old mattresses, giving the house a good clean for the next group (I recommend hiring someone for this as it can be daunting), even painting rooms in some cases. Kitchen appliances usually need a major clean and some landlords have been known to simply buy a used stove/fridge combo rather than tackle cleaning the existing units. Used appliances can be had for $250 or less at second-hand stores on Barton Street.

Thanks to the way the schools run, students are often still writing exams the day before they're supposed to leave your house. If you have a new group of kids arriving May 1st for example, you may want to ensure the house is empty first. A lot of landlords don't want to be at the house during the transition day-somehow feeling the kids will sort it out.

That only leads to complaints and that's not the way you want to start your relationship with new tenants.

Seasoned landlords will sign leases with either May 2nd as the start date or May 1st after 6pm. This is difficult to execute unless you are physically there yourself and often students from out-of-town will insist on moving in the day before if possible. On the bright side, often students leaving will depart a few days prior to the end of the lease unless they are writing exams. Simple communication will allow you to know what to expect come May 1st and/or September 1st, the first days of semester.

Your tenants should have all their own furniture, usually consisting of a bed, desk and set of dresser drawers. Most landlords furnish the common area with either a table and chairs, couch, even a television (not hooked up to cable), but if you don't, the tenants may pick up cheap items for the house. When showing rooms to prospective tenants, a furnished kitchen and common area go a long way to attract students.

If you're going after international students, you might consider furnishing the rooms (bed, desk, drawers) and advertising such. Often these students are only looking for furnished rooms as they don't have time or physical ability to furnish prior to moving in.

If your tenants are first-year, you will often meet the parents when they move in and this is a good time to spark a relationship with them should their son or daughter become a problem later on. It's also a good time to ask them to sign a guarantor letter if you haven't already done so on your lease.

Returning students are usually on their own by second year; parents having miraculously disappeared. They are more seasoned, less demanding, and easy to convince of the need for organized chore schedules. The downside is that their parents often refuse to guarantee at this point. Get details about the student's work place (most have part-time jobs by now), so that you can consider garnisheeing if it comes to that. Remember though that if a student is in that much dire straights, they will likely quit the job and go home anyway.

# Signing a lease

Students and Landlords are protected by the Landlord and Tenant Act, a copy of which can be easily obtained online. You can ask a lawyer to write up a good lease for you (expensive), or you can ask another Landlord neighbour to give you a copy of theirs. Or you can ask a real estate agent who specializes in buying and selling student houses to provide you with one their clients use. If you would like a sample of the one I use, drop me an email (at back of book) and I'll be happy to send one along.

Certain things can go in a lease and other things cannot.
For example, requesting a safety deposit is illegal and would not stand up in court. Insisting that tenants not have pets is equally as illegal though the word *request* can often be written in such a manner that the students assume the house is a no-pet environment. You can use terminology relating to allergies, safety, insurance, etc. to convince them that pets are not a good idea. But if a student brings one with them, you cannot legally get rid of it, or them, unless it presents a danger to one or more of the other tenants. If a tenant decides to have their boyfriend or girlfriend move in, technically it is not against the law unless you can get the

insurance company or mortgage lender to state, in writing, that coverage is null and void if more than X number of tenants are living in the home.

Long, exhaustive leases are not necessary as both parties are covered by the Landlord Tenant Act, provided the essentials of a contract are adhered to:

1) names of both parties
2) address of property, contact info for landlord
3) price of room, length of lease
4) who pays utilities
5) what happens if they decide to leave prior to the end of the lease
6) what happens if they destroy or harm the property
7) what happens if they have a friend move in with them
8) signature of both parties, dated
9) signature of guarantor, along with contact info, dated
10) amount of money required to have the lease take effect. This is usually first and last month's rent, however, to make the document legal instantly, you may request a deposit of a few hundred dollars.

Note this in the lease.

Remember that only when money changes hands is your lease a legal contract. If you don't receive money at signing and the tenant later changes his/her mind, you cannot go after them unless some amount of money has transferred between parties.

In Hamilton, one of the by-laws which often arises when dealing with student houses is the multiple-lease law. Technically, if you have more than one lease on your property, you are running a multi-residential property, or lodging house. The laws regarding these types of properties are considerably different to what you actually want.

The way around this by-law is to create one lease for the home (thereby satisfying the statement that one family is living in the home). Have the total amount of rent listed on the lease but refer to Schedule A for each tenant. Then on individual Schedule A's, list the individual tenant's info. Include name, property address, rent due including utilities if you are doing it that way, email and phone numbers for the tenant and their parents, a description of which room they will be occupying (create a drawing of the home, depicting where rooms are and numbering them, if you wish, and call it Schedule B), and signatures, dated.

You will have a master lease for the whole amount and that is the one you would show the City if they request it. You would also have Schedule A's and B's for each room in your home (which you don't give to the City unless they request it). Give a copy of the master lease plus one pertinent Schedule A/B to each tenant. You do not have to give each tenant copies of the other tenants' Schedules.

If you write your lease this way, you will have to change one standard clause which is referred to in this notice from McMaster University's Off-Campus housing office:

*Under most tenancy agreements, if you all appear on the same lease, you are each responsible to the landlord for the whole rent. Your obligation to the landlord is referred to as being "joint and several" in nature. If one of your housemates fails to pay their share of the rent, the landlord can look to the remaining housemates to make up the difference and will be in a position to begin eviction proceedings. It would then be your responsibility to pursue the defaulting housemate for their share of the rent. (It is best to seek legal advice concerning potential actions by the landlord and your rights against the defaulting housemate. Contact the Off-Campus Resource Centre for details about who to contact for legal advice.)*

This notice is given to every new student registering at the school as part of the introductory package. Most landlords using the Schedule A type of lease remove this clause (or ones worded similarly) as it would not be binding since you are not providing the entire lease to each tenant. It also means that if one tenant skips out on the lease, you cannot go to the others to make up the difference, unless you are dealing with a group of friends at a discounted rate, in which case you might.

Although a common practice with families in multi-housing units, it does not work for student housing as many tenants do not know their co-tenants and would never agree to be responsible for their mistakes.

A lawyer would give you advice on this but it has been used enough times for me to tell you that you would never get such a statement enforced should you take a bunch of tenants to court anyway.

All issues between Landlords and Tenants are dealt with at the Tribunal, operated in Ontario by the Landlord and Tenant Board. As stated on their website (<http://www.sjto.gov.on.ca/ltb/>):

127

*"The Landlord and Tenant Board (LTB) resolves disputes between residential landlords and tenants, and eviction applications filed by non-profit housing co-operatives.*
*The LTB also provides information about its practices and procedures and the rights and responsibilities of landlords and tenants under the Residential Tenancies Act.*

The Board has a tendency to lean toward the rights of the tenant more than the Landlord but if your complaint is clear and legally sound, you will win your case. Each party usually represents themselves, thereby eliminating the cost of legal counsel.

Many landlords find it simpler, however, to just remove troublesome or non-paying tenants and replace them with new tenants. You may lose one or two month's rent, but that may be cheaper than taking the original tenant to court, especially if that tenant has now disappeared.

One story of a tribunal decision going against a Landlord concerns the common area. When renting his home, the landlord showed seven bedrooms, a kitchen, and a living room common area. The kids signed a lease based on that dynamic. Part way through the year, the landlord decided to turn the common area into another bedroom. The tenants took the landlord to the tribunal stating they enjoyed the space and that the lease specified only seven rooms. The landlord was forced to re-establish the common area. He was also fined $2500 and had to pay the tenants' legal fees.

Had the landlord waited until the lease was finished, then added a new room, and changed his lease to state eight rooms, he would have been within his rights to do so. Doing it while an existing lease was in place was clearly breaking the Landlord/Tenant relationship according to the Board.

On the other side of the coin, when a student claimed the house was too noisy and he wasn't going to pay his rent until the Landlord solved the problem, the Tribunal decided in the Landlord's favour, forcing the tenant to pay past and current rents. The Landlord was then advised to solve the problem to the satisfaction of all tenants or face a review of the finding.

The cost of going the tribunal route is not as expensive, complicated, or as time consuming as small claims court, so keep in mind that tenants are not intimidated by the process. Of course, it's cheaper for you also and was put in place to essentially allow tenants and landlords to settle disputes without financing such actions being a major issue.

If you are leasing to first year students, you will likely have parental involvement. In this case, obtaining a guarantor signature is usually not difficult. However, second year students onward are usually fending for themselves for the most part and obtaining a parental signature is difficult. Often, the kids will provide an email address for you to send documentation to, have a signature applied, and returned to you. Unfortunately, these email addresses are often set up by the tenant for just that purpose and the signature you have on file is their forgery of a parental signature.

Older students also resent the fact that you require a parental approval. They are starting out on their own and want to enter into, and be responsible for, their own contracts. Most students are honest. You only hear about the negligent or deceitful ones.

It is also difficult to run credit checks on students as most are only beginning to establish themselves and there is little to go on. Better to obtain info including family home address (in case you need to mail registered legal documents), job information, school studies, etc. (so you can reach them on campus if necessary). Credit checks on parents are useless unless they are listed as guarantors. Most parents will resent your doing so if they find out, however, as any check counts as a hit against their credit rating.

Finally, ensure that each tenant has a copy of the lease or master lease and pertinent personal Schedules as no lease can be enforced if the tenant doesn't have a copy. I suggest you have them sign for it, or at least keep a record of an email sent, as they can easily say they did not receive a copy during a dispute.

Student Housing

# Chapter Four:
# The Investor

# Why do people sell?

"If student housing is such a great investment, why would people want to sell?"

As an agent, this is a question I am asked regularly. Why would someone want to divest of such a great investment? The answers are many and often don't have anything to do with ROI. Many investors are actually parents who purchased a home so their own child(ren) could attend school. Upon graduation, they choose whether to maintain the investment or sell because they don't need it anymore. About 50% of those people do sell, primarily because they don't live in the area (the reason they bought it in the first place), and find it too difficult to manage from a distance. Others in this category keep the property for a while, realize it is too much for them to manage, and sell at a later date.

Other investors have Five or Ten Year Plans. In other words, they justify the investment by including the resale price as part of the final ROI, incorporating appreciation. These are investors who will carry a home with even or negative cash flow, anticipating all the ROI upon resale. Admittedly, this is not a popular method and most investors

134

shy away from negative cash flow properties, and usage of appreciation, but since the increase in value of student homes is far superior to any other type of investment property at the moment, their logic is tough to argue.

Other investors simply get tired of working with young people and multiple-room rentals. It is challenging to deal with seven or eight individuals (which is why many investors seek out groups of friends), ensuring income is steady and on time. Repairs and renovations are also a factor. Contrary to popular belief, students to not destroy properties. They are, however, very hard on them. Dishes are often left in sinks and on counters. Posters, notes, etc. are often posted on walls of rooms, leaving holes everywhere. Floors are never cleaned, doors are often pulled off hinges, bathrooms are never clean, and the very fact that eight people are living in a home simply wears out everything from floors to bathtubs to carpeting.

For some investors, the headache of constantly maintaining the property is too much. They prefer to deal with single family tenants in a regular rental unit. Of course, the ROI is lower but the headaches are less.

A lot of investors put no money into their properties, aiming to sell them in five years or so at a profit. These homes are usually tired, in dire need of upgrades and repairs, but since they continue to provide cash flow, the owners simply ignore to address any issues. They know full well that another investor will buy the home and either repeat the process or spend money on the home. Either way, his ROI will be 15% per year or higher.

Again, popular to common belief, the City does not spend a lot of time searching out slum lords and slum properties. In fact, unless a complaint is received, a compliance officer will likely never visit the home. The few homes that make the news as degenerate and unsafe properties are discovered because a neighbour or tenant has complained to the City. In Hamilton, the budget for compliance officers is not high enough to warrant a constant presence; they are too busy in the East and North ends of the City where slum properties are more prevalent.

And finally, because the price of entry is so high, many investors feel they can put their money to better use elsewhere. This is questionable but enough investors feel that way that virtually every 3-5 years, you'll see myriad listings go up in the Westdale/Ainslie Woods area. These investors have put 20% down and have run a minimal cash flow for the duration. When they sell, they stand to make upwards of $50,000 (on avg) on that investment. However, they have to wait the five years to get it and there is little monthly income for the period.

Other investments which don't require a 20% down payment, will provide a lower return but in a shorter period of time. Many investors of this ilk feel they make more money on volume deals than they do in holding on to properties for five or more years. Of course, a good portion of these investors are also licensed real estate agents, having procured the license for the express purpose of selling their homes and saving the commissions (which can indeed amount to 25% of the gross profit in some cases).

As an agent, my motto has always been that when one investor has decided he/she has maximized their investment, another investor sees an opportunity to begin maximizing theirs. I have sold addresses multiple times in the past decade and each investor has made money on the sale; many on the cash flow also. Those homes often have had no upgrades or repairs (other than essential) from owner to owner, but continue to increase in value at a rate of 15% per year (on avg.), making it appealing to each new generation of investor. Many of these homes were built between 1890 and 1970, so you can imagine how many times they have been turned over. An alarming number of those homes also still look like they did when they were first built.

# Timing of Sales

More than any other type of real estate investment, the timing of a student home sale is critical. Despite this, homes are available for sale all year round. You will find, however, that during the months of April, May and Sept, Oct, there are a lot more properties available.

The simple reason for this is that tenants are either leaving and not coming back, or are entering into new leases. This is the ideal time for an owner to divest of a property because the house will either be empty on the first day of the next semester, or full of brand new tenants.

There are debates over which time is best, and a lot depends upon who the buyer of your property will eventually be. If a family is looking for a home for their own child(ren), then they are looking for a home that will be empty when they buy.

The majority of buyers, however, are investors, and as such, a fully-tenanted home has more value to them. So much so, in fact, that the house can be priced higher if all the rooms are leased for a full term (1 year).

The dilemma, of course, is deciding which buyer you will attract. And that's very difficult to ascertain. Even families looking for homes for their kids beginning in May will begin shopping as early as December the prior year.

The best thing to do is to play the odds. You will sell the home for a higher price if you are listed when most of the other homes are listed. That is anytime from Feb-May and again Sept-Nov. If you have kids with signed leases in place, you will be more attractive to investors. You should be able to demand a higher price for a fully-leased home but the market often proves that theory wrong. Some investors are experienced at finding tenants and actually want to choose their own, so they prefer empty homes. If you are not charging the going rate for rents, it can actually be a deterrent to selling as the new owner has to honour whatever leases you have in place if they buy your home. If an investor feels your rooms are worth more than you're charging, he may move on to a more lucrative property.

Sometimes, the owner is disillusioned and simply wants out. Perhaps they've had a bad batch of tenants this year and can't take the headache anymore. Perhaps the home needs some repairs/upgrades and they don't want to put out the money. Or perhaps, they find the process of finding new tenants every twelve to twenty-four months too daunting to continue.

Some owners sell their home when the mortgage is due in order to avoid penalties which can be very high. Much of the profit can be lost to banks if you don't time your sale accordingly. If the home is on the market past your renewal date, consider a short-term mortgage to carry you to a sale. Penalties will be considerably lower.

And then there are those with the five-year plans. They have been making money from cash flow and now want to increase their ROI by cashing in on the home's increased value. They know that selling in the Spring or early Fall is when the most buyers will be out there shopping. They also know that inventory will be higher at this time but if they believe they have priced their property correctly, it will be a better buy than the others and they will sell quickly and for top dollar.

You'll note I didn't say the most money in the least amount of time. That is because many five-year plan investors have no intention of repairing major issues with the home. They take what they can for their term, then sell at an appropriate price. That price may be slightly lower than competitors because the home needs some work. It doesn't matter. Some investors look for those homes and as long as you hold out for a fair price, you will get it.

For those selling homes that their own children occupied during their tenure as students, note that often they are in much better condition than an investor's home. Parents often do many of the overdue repairs and also upgrade the homes to suit their perception of the level of living their child is accustomed to. Often, they want to recoup some of that investment upon selling and, as such, they overprice the homes for the investor market. These homes will often sit on the market for a month or two and then either be reduced or the owner will accept a more reasonable market price offer from an investor. In some rare cases, another family will purchase it and be happy to pay the premium for a more suitable home for their child.

Of course, every year, homes that have been completely updated, and are fully leased for the next term, are breaking sales records, and for that there seems to be no end.
It is better to have a good product on the market because you can then set your price at the top of the market when

selling. There are always buyer's out there as student housing continues to be a great investment, despite the price of entry.

# What improvements are you looking for?

When you're looking for a home for your family, you look for certain comforts that suit your needs and your standard of living. When considering rental investments, much of those things are also considered, though perhaps the level of living may be acceptable if a little lower. Such things as older appliances, laminate floors, cheaper paint, etc., are all things you would consider for a rental property.

Student housing is different. Although we don't want the homes to be hovels, we also don't want them to resemble hotel accommodations. Often kitchens in student homes are either the original ones or are only slightly updated (appliances mostly). Flooring is preferably inexpensive laminate as it wears better than hardwood and is easier to clean than carpet.

Bathrooms are usually upgraded as they get intense use. Nothing fancy, just shower stalls and tougher fixtures. Sometimes the water heater is changed for one with more capacity. Rooms will need painting at least once every two semesters. Kids hang up posters, pin things to walls, etc., and they become very worn very quickly.

144

No one repairs an entire roof but rather adds shingles when required and only where required. Likewise, no major landscaping is done as it is completely lost on students and they won't offer to maintain it for you anyway.

Decks and balconies are sometimes found on homes but they were usually put in when the property was still a family home.

It is law that a smoke detector must be located outside every bedroom and at least one carbon monoxide detector on each floor. Building code is changing to enforce wired-in detection systems but at time of writing, battery operated detectors were still sufficient. A quick call to the Building Department at City Hall will clarify that point for you.

Most investors find that they are replacing floors, bathrooms, and paint at least once every three to five years. Roofs about every ten. Appliances are often changed every year or two and purchased from second hand outlets. It is often cheaper to replace them than clean them.

The reason so little upgrades are done in student homes is *not* that there is a blatant disregard for their well-being: Quite the contrary; most landlords are very conscious about providing a safe, healthy environment for their young tenants. However, granite countertops and new cabinetry don't really have a place here. The aesthetics are lost on most of the students and the wear and tear on these materials can be substantial. Imagine eight teenagers living in your home. That's what a student house is really like.

Your goal is to make sure the home is safe and to make sure it is easy for the tenants to maintain. A quick sweep of floors, and the occasional wipe down of the kitchen counter is about all you can expect from most student tenants.

There are, of course, some investors who disagree with this and they do upgrade the homes in an attempt to attract better quality tenants. The jury is out in my mind as to how successful this approach is. One or two of my clients have upgraded their homes but their rent rates are no higher than other clients who have not. I do agree that it is likely easier to rent out a nicer looking facility, but does the cost justify the results?

My one client who has gone to extreme lengths to upgrade his home (granite counters, glass backsplash, stainless-steel appliances, televisions, leather couches, etc.), and has had tremendous success attracting first year students. Parents

146

love his facility and he often has tenants stay for their full term. His home is right under the escarpment, however, and he felt he needed something extra to attract people to live that far away from school. His rents are no higher than other homes on the same street. He does not, however, spend as much time as they do on filling his rooms each year. To him, that's justification enough.

When savvy investors compare student homes they look at the infrastructure; the things that are going to cost them the most to ensure a safe and cost-effective environment for their tenants.

Roofing, furnace, windows, water heater, siding, eaves, etc. are all items the investor does not want to spend money on (unless he's getting a bargain on the buy). Those are the things you should be worrying about when you buy, and those are the things you should be considering when pricing your home to sell. If you don't want to replace these items when selling, that's fine, but you'll have to price your property accordingly. Many investors have had homes sit on the market for several months just because they had original windows, for example. If they had accepted a reduced offer, or replaced windows and maintained a fair market price, this would not occur. Student homes in Hamilton are very similar. The only thing distinguishing them are: 1) the number of rooms, and 2) the condition of the infrastructure. Pricing a student home is almost entirely reliant upon those two considerations.

# The different types of Investors

We've touched on this previously in Chapter Two and if you're reading this, you are most likely an investor. And you probably fit into one of four categories:

1)      You have a child who is going to attend, is currently attending, or has graduated from McMaster University or Columbia College.

2)      You are an investor with a portfolio centred around real estate holdings and are looking for a certain return on investment over a short or long term

3)      You are part of a group of investors who park funds in various channels, one of which is real estate.

4)      You are a seeking a way to supplement your retirement income by having positive cash flow from investments that don't require a lot of involvement or maintenance.

Each investor category has different requirements and expectations. And although the product is essentially the same (single family homes used as student residences), individual properties are better suited to some categories more than others.

Let's look at the parent investor firstly.

A parent is looking for a safe, clean environment for their child. Usually, they want the house to be close to campus, so the child can easily walk to school. If the family is accustomed to a certain level of living, then the parent is looking to duplicate that as best as possible in the student residence.

Most parents understand that student housing is not going to look or feel like single family living, but they want to get as close as they can. In some cases, they're even willing to upgrade and renovate the right home to bring it to a satisfactory level. Please note that the child is usually not included in conversations about the condition of the house. Often, they don't care or at very least, have no experience as they are usually first-year students or second year students who spent their first year in residence on campus.

Parents don't want to lose money. And they are usually interested in making money in the long run. However, it is not their primary motivation. Safety, cleanliness, and proximity are. If a real estate agent can convince a parent that their child will essentially live for free over the course of their studies (thanks to other tenant friends who will be paying the mortgage), and that they are virtually guaranteed to make money when selling the home four to six years later, then the decision is not that difficult. In fact, if the parent is convinced that there is money to be made, they can justify the expense of upgrading the home to their (not their child's) preferences.

Often, the parent will hold onto the home after the child has graduated and moved on, for the simple reason that the positive cash flow-or assurance of a high ROI upon selling-is too good to lose. Without a child living in the home, however, many of these parents realize that being a landlord to strangers is not as easy as operating a house where their son or daughter acts as house manager. That's why a large number of homes purchased by parents are sold 5-8 years after initial purchase.

One of the more significant factors about parent investing is that they will often consider homes that investors will not. In other words, if a home is over-priced, in poor condition, or has only 3 or 4 rentable rooms, investors will shun them. For a parent, however, these homes are often ideal. They are not necessarily looking for high ROIs or even positive cash flow. They are looking for proximity, safety, and an enjoyable lifestyle for their child. These are all things that a savvy investor has no interest in. The average investor home has a minimum of 6-10 rentable rooms, is located further away from the school, and is maximized for use (in other words, there is likely not a living room, landscaped back yard, or empty garage).

A savvy parent will realize that if they intend to sell the home later, they should consider these things in order for the home to appeal to investors, but many simply don't think that far ahead.

Of important note concerning this type of investor, financing is not as difficult a proposition as any of the other categories. If a family member is going to live in the home then high down payments are not as essential, interest rates are more reasonable, and mortgages more easily obtained. Lenders still perceive the purchase as an investment but don't consider the risk factor high because the renter will not be a third party. However they justify it internally, banks feel their risk is lower when a family member is living in the home. If that family member is also on title with the parent, the banking doors seem to swing wide open.

The second type of investor is someone who has invested in real estate before. Perhaps they came into money when their parents passed, or perhaps they are simply very good at manipulating other people's money (banks, friends, relatives, etc.). Student Housing is not usually the first real estate vehicle they will look at. Single family rental properties are usually accomplished first, or even rentals of their personal properties after moving up.

Often they hear about student housing from the plethora of investment groups that abound in every major Canadian city. Author, Don Campbell runs a very successful group of Toronto investors and has influenced many of them who have eventually purchased in the Greater Hamilton area. His formulas for ROI are easily recognizable and many student home investors follow his teachings in order to succeed in this particular niche. He is, of course, only one of many.

This type of investor almost always uses leveraged funds with down payments coming from inheritances, re-financing of homes, or business loans (from friends, banks, lender groups, etc.).

Expectations are very high, and formulas are often adhered to, despite the quickly changing marketplace. Once integrated into the environment, however, some are able to realize that profits can be had if they work with good partners such as real estate agents experienced in student housing, second tier lenders who have funded student housing before, and mortgage brokers who understand the nuances of dealing with lenders who are open to student home investments.

Without the proper advice from the above professionals, many investors in this category have made serious mistakes and have ultimately experienced major financial losses.

Many feel that their high credit rating, low exposure, and strong relationship with major banks is enough for them to enter the student house market. Nothing could be further from the truth. The big banks don't like student housing. Their reasoning is completely outdated but that is irrelevant. If investors in this category rely on their relationships with banks that centre around *normal* experiences (normal being traditionally accepted investment channels sanctioned by banks), then they become disillusioned very quickly. At time of print only one major Canadian bank will even consider a student house mortgage (Royal) but even they require a 30% down payment. As an investment based on leveraged funds, a 30% down payment is ludicrous.

Federal law states that an investment property requires a minimum 20% down payment. Some new investors attempt to circumvent this rule, and in other types of rental investments, they can often achieve that goal. With student housing, however, this is virtually impossible. In fact, many investors will establish credit lines based on other criteria (home valuations, employment statistics, other non-real estate investments, etc.) and then purchase the homes on that credit line. They will attempt to re-finance at a later date when the property has increased in value and their equity is considerably higher. You need an accountant to explain this of course as both the laws and the dynamics of this type of financing change constantly.

Most investors in this category are looking at a three to five-year investment period. They purchase a home with minimal positive cash flow but account for the annual value increases when formulating their end goal ROI. Most investment groups shun this type of thinking, which is why many new investors shy away from student housing. In years gone by, high positive cash flow was possible and returns of 8-10% were feasible without including profits from resale as part of the annual ROI. Of late, however, the cost of entry has increased so much that zero or low cash flow is acceptable, creating annual ROIs of 3-4%. When the property is sold at the end of the three to five-year term, the appreciation is integrated into the annual calculations and ROIs of 8-15% per annum are then realized. No other investment relies so heavily upon resale profits. And the only reason student housing succeeds this way is because the market is completely sustainable. There will always be students and they will always require housing. Regardless of what the rest of the City is experiencing, student housing is constantly increasing in value; basic supply and demand in a perfect environment.

Group investors are rare in student housing but they do have more access to funding. Private lenders, REITs, and other partnerships are often formed specifically to invest in student housing. The critical, and often deciding factor however, is that one of the partners has to be involved in maintaining the home. Student housing is not a hands-off investment unless you're willing to hire property managers. Most groups frown on additional costs such as management, especially when there are so many individuals involved.

The most successful groups are a combination of the money guy, the maintenance guy, and the property guy. The latter is often a real estate agent or property manager who will provide hands-on, regular interaction with the tenants. The money guy handles getting funds based on the group's combined exposure. The maintenance guy is sometimes a contractor who renovates, upgrades, and maintains the property. The division of responsibility and profits varies. The biggest problem this type of investor has is group consensus. The successful ones have one or at most two people choosing the property. If more people are involved, it usually never happens.

Student housing is simply not black and white and it's certainly not just about the numbers. Students themselves create a dynamic in the equation that demands attention. They are the factor that will make or break your investment. A lot of group investors aren't interested in getting that close to the action and therefore defer to other vehicles. In fact, some members of these groups buy out the partners and become members of another category of investor.

Perhaps the most prominent of investors is the person who is seeking a way to supplement retirement income. They may have inherited money from their parents, or recently been downsized and received a buy-out package. Some have realized that the equity in their own family home is so large, they can easily borrow against it or even establish a large credit line.

Regardless of where the money comes from, this type of investor is usually hands-on, not afraid to deal with young tenants, and equally un-afraid to do a little renovating around an investment property.

Student housing is ideal for this type of investor. The cash flow from a student house can supplement retirement income tremendously, especially if the investment is planned and purchased well in advance of retirement itself. If a mortgage can be substantially decreased during your work years, then the income generated from a student house is usually far greater than a regular income property. Homes that were purchased ten years ago are now worth double their original sticker price and now that those owners are ready to retire they face the very real possibility that they have created the ultimate retirement plan. They can continue to supplement with monthly rents, or they can sell the property for a substantial profit, and invest that money into other vehicles.

Most, however, recognize that student housing is likely the best vehicle anyway and simply hang on to the properties. I've spoken with some folks in their retirement years who are thrilled that they can enjoy the fruits of their investment now, but can also pass on the property to family as their inheritance.

Oddly enough, student homes owned by this type of investor are often the best run operations on their streets. Since the owners are retired, they spend time tinkering with minor repairs, upgrades, etc. They also have parental relationships with the tenants who respond in kind and take good care of the property. And, most importantly, they tend to achieve the highest rents per room and the highest fill capacity. Many are local residents which makes visiting the house regularly simpler, but not all. One of my Toronto clients has two houses in Hamilton and is here twice per week fiddling with things and getting to know his tenants. They have taken to calling him "Pops".

# Turnkey, Reno—Upgrade, Update

There are basically four types of student homes you, as an investor, can consider: the turnkey operation, the slum-lord house, the tired renovation project, and the residential home.

The first is a turnkey operation. The previous owner has kept the house in good condition and probably has all the rooms leased out for the upcoming semester. In some cases, if the home is currently owned by a parent whose child recently graduated, they may try to sell the home vacant, assuming other parents will want an empty house in which to place their own child(ren) and their friends.

If a parent owned the home previously, you'll likely find they did some upgrades that perhaps you, as an investor, would not have spent the money on. For example, many parents feel the kids need a new kitchen (because that's what they're used to at home), an elaborate common room, complete with TV, furnishings, and built-in bookshelves, etc.

When they sell the home, they try to recoup some of that expenditure in the sale price and the market usually tells them it won't work but it takes time. If you're looking at a parent's home when it first comes on the market, you'll find the price may be higher than comparable homes. Unless you're emotionally attached to it, wait for a couple of weeks. When the parents realize they've overpriced the home (hopefully they hired a knowledgeable student house agent), then the price will come down for you. Of course, you could always try a lower price right away. Often parents will work with the first buyer who shows interest because they just want to be rid of the property.

Surprisingly, otherwise savvy business people don't see their child's residence as a positive investment. They've saved money on accommodations for the child's tenure, so they're happy. Making a hefty profit off the sale of that home is not vital. After all, they probably need the money to buy that same child their first car, first and last month's rent, etc.

These homes are, in fact, worth a few extra dollars because they are in better condition than comparable homes. They will attract a better quality tenant and you may be able to charge a higher rent.

There are, of course, some investors who treat their homes as if their own children live there. These homes will not appear as upgraded as a parent home but the infrastructure will be newer. Things like bathrooms, roofing, furnaces, windows, etc. will all be upgraded. When these homes come on to the market, they are priced high and often go into bidding wars. If you want an existing, well-run turnkey student home, these are the ones to ask your Realtor® to look for. You will, however, pay top dollar for them.

These are all things to consider when weighing the cost of a turnkey home to one of the other types.

At the other end of the scale is the slum lord home. These are student houses that have been in existence for several years, likely owned by several investors. Usually, very little has been done to the home over the years and it has just been a money maker for its owners.

You, of course, may want to continue that trend and, within reason, you can consider that option. As long as the home is safe, rooms are a decent size, and the rent is appropriate, then major renovations may be avoided for another few semesters.

Most people, however, when facing a home that has had no upgrades or repairs for several years, will feel the need to improve the facility, and not just for altruistic reasons. Homes which appear modern and safe will attract a better tenant, faster. Those tenants are also more likely to pay a little more for better accommodations.

What makes the older student home different to any other fixer-upper is that the reno's you consider only need to meet the standards of a young person who spends most of his or her time at the school. What that means is that you don't need granite counters, backsplash, modern appliances, etc. What you need is the necessities. Spend money upgrading the bathrooms. Add a shower in the basement if you can. Bathrooms are where students spend a lot of time when home. And, of course, they all want to shower at the same time. Some of the older homes on King St., (one of the streets running from McMaster to Westdale Village), have three showers in the basement, not full bathrooms, just extra showers. Due to their age and size, there may only be one or two bedrooms down there but students on the upper floors don't mind going into the basement to shower if one is available. So lining up shower rooms like a dormitory is not a bad idea, as long as you upgrade the water heater while you're at it. Consider the new waterless heaters. They are much smaller units that heat water as it is brought into the house as opposed to keeping a portion of water warm in a tank.

Don't spend money on appliances. Students don't really use them. A good, large microwave is a good idea; maybe even two of them. Ovens are used to heat up pizza's and get dirty very quickly. Stove tops are almost never used except for bacon and eggs on weekends, etc. Some international students, notably Chinese, will cook extensively, so keep that in mind when renting to other nationalities.

New appliances will be ruined. Better to buy second-hand ones or simply keep repairing the old ones that came with the house. There are several second-hand appliance stores along Barton Street in Central Hamilton and Concession Street on the mountain where you can pick up perfectly workable fridges and stoves for a couple of hundred dollars each.

The best investment you can make is to put down laminate flooring everywhere. It's easy to clean, inexpensive, and when it gets tired looking, can be easily replaced. Carpeting harbours odours and gets dirty looking very quickly. If you have any water leakage in your basement (especially in the older Westdale homes), carpeting will absorb the moisture and become not only dirty and smelly but dangerously full of mould also.

The third type of student home is the mid-range renovation project. These homes are the most common. They have been successful student homes in the past and have had some upgrades over the years but now appear tired. Paint is peeling, kitchens and baths need newer reno's, and the owner hasn't maximized use of space.

Student housing is not an investment where bargain hunters survive, mostly because those investing in this vehicle are educated sellers and know exactly what their homes are worth. Having said that, many who are ready to take their profits out are willing to give you a fair price for a property they have looked after for five to ten years. You aren't going to get the price lowered because of the upgrades required but you will usually get a fair price.

Ask your Realtor® for the names of renovators in the area who specialize in student housing. These guys understand the vehicle and will quote based on lower-priced, medium quality materials that will last a minimum of five years. Laminate flooring, paint, base off-the-shelf units (shower stalls, vanities, etc.) will look new and modern but likely wouldn't be the same quality of materials you would put in your own home.

You'll be amazed at what a good coat of paint will achieve. A tired home comes alive when painted, especially if the laminate flooring is clean and polished. Many of these renovators are also able to do minor plumbing and electrical too though they usually aren't licensed to do so. A lot depends upon your comfort level with tradespeople. If you want the reno's cheap, it can be done by a single contractor (and he will do it to meet building code) but he may not be able to offer warranties, etc., because he isn't licensed for various aspects of the work. Fully licensed contractors will be more expensive, and they usually aren't used to cutting corners on materials, etc., but that may suit your comfort level better.

Over the years, the use of space has changed when it comes to student housing also. In the 1990's, for example, having a large common area was required in order to attract students. They would set up a TV for video games, perhaps have a dining room table set up, or a living room set up with couches and chairs. Parties were common and the space was used as a gathering point for friends.

During the first part of the new millennium, things changed a little. School got harder, costs went up for students and, as a result, the party atmosphere dwindled. Kids were spending more time in their rooms studying and weren't apt to utilize a common area as much. Local restaurants and clubs were offering facilities and events that catered to the students and the homes were becoming less and less the meeting place for entertainment.

Savvy landlords during this period decided to maximize the space of the homes and began turning living rooms and dining rooms into bedrooms. In exchange, they would provide better kitchen areas by adding small tables, breakfast bars, and even TVs, but they would add a couple of rooms to the house, thereby increasing income.

Students didn't seem to mind the gradual change, especially if the landlord rented rooms one at a time (as opposed to a group of friends). For many of the smaller homes, this change turned the investment from a neutral to a positive cash flow situation.

As of the 2013 semester, we noticed a change back to the common area again, necessitated by students being more social; not partying, but more congregational. Although it hasn't taken full hold as of 2016 (time of print), many homes are reverting at least one main floor bedroom back into a common area. Part of the reasoning is the growth of video gaming. But also, the congregational nature of students has increased and study groups, project groups, and the like, need places to gather and common areas of their residences are ideal. We have also noticed that groups of friends are more common again (there was a waning of this phenomenon during the early part of the new millennium) and such groups welcome a place where they can congregate.

Keep in mind that whenever you make any changes to your property, there must either be no leases in place, or you have written consent from all tenants that they are in agreement with the change. If you make arbitrary changes to accommodations during a lease period, the tenants have every right to demand you change it back and are aware that the Tenant/Landlord Tribunal will agree with them.

The final type of property is the residential home. There are not many left in the Westdale/Ainslie Woods area, and when they are listed for sale, you can guarantee you will be facing a bidding war with other like-minded investors. Residential homes are, by their nature, in better condition and often incorporate upgrades that are lost on students. However, many of the older, majestic homes have the potential to become 8-10 bedroom facilities and are, therefore, very profitable, despite their high cost.

When considering the purchase of a home that is currently a family home, you are likely looking at a three or four-bedroom property. Turning living, dining, den, and basement recreation rooms into additional bedrooms requires a vision and some renovation funds. Most large basements can house three or four bedrooms and a bathroom. Most living/dining rooms can become a bedroom/common room set up. By law, renovating a home in this manner should be done with a permit but many investors skip that part and simply do the retro-fitting without permission. We'll discuss this more in depth later but suffice to say that a major renovation of a family home is usually difficult to keep off the radar and so the City will no doubt pay a visit at some point during the renovation period.

When a residence is turned into a student home, this is the point when it's value will be the highest. No students have lived here yet and it is now maximized for a large number of students. Selling at this point will garner the highest price. If you lease the home to students prior to listing, you will attract the turnkey buyer and your home will appear better than any competitor's. Some "flip" investors have made a lot of money in the past on these properties, though as mentioned, they are so infrequently listed now that the original buying price is usually very high. Quick profits on a flip are considerably difficult to obtain so many flippers are now holding onto the properties for a year or so until the property appreciates in value naturally. As long as the home cash flows neutrally at least during this period, the flippers are content to wait it out.

# Why you need an agent

## For Buyers

It will sound like a sales pitch of course but I'm not bias... really.

You need an agent for student housing for some very sound reasons, the most important being that a lot of the listings are only located on the MLS® meaning that if you drive around the neighbourhood, you will miss a lot of them because there are no signs on the lawns.

Owners are often selling the home while tenants are still living there. Tenants get nervous when a *For Sale* sign is in front of their house. It's also difficult to convince them that their lease will remain intact regardless of who owns the house (if selling mid-term).

Getting tenants to work with you when selling a house is a challenge sometimes. The kids don't like interruptions when studying and don't understand that they have no choice. They demand 24 hours notice of showings (which is the law) and often don't clean up the house prior to showings.

Seasoned investors understand this but for those who are uninitiated, it can be a rude awakening.

If you have an agent with you, often they will already know the kids, or at the very least, be familiar with the house (having shown or sold it before). The agent also takes all the flak from the tenants as well as the Seller should they complain after your visit.

But primarily, the agent is privy to new listings long before they hit the MLS®. Student housing is very specialized and the agents that work in the medium understand the nuances, including being aware of new listings before they are even put up for sale. Many agents sell their own client's homes and, if possible, will do it privately to save their Sellers money on commissions. If you are working with one of these agents, you will be privy to all those "pocket" listings ahead of time and will be allowed to make an offer.

Once a home is listed on the MLS® it becomes a free-for-all. Buyers from all over the GTA as well as parents from anywhere in the country are getting listing feeds from their agents telling them when a new property comes up for sale. As a result, there will be many showings in the first couple of days (about one day before the listing hits the public MLS® system) and it is sold. Often, several buyers are interested and the home is sold during a bidding war, usually for thousands above the list price.

Agents specializing in student housing are well versed in the strategies and techniques required to wade these waters without drowning. They will make sure you don't spend too much for a property, or waste time in a bidding war you can never win. Most importantly, they will send you listings the second they go up for sale. In such a highly specialized market niche with investors all looking for the same thing, you need a partner who can steer you in the right direction, at the right time, and for the right price.

Agents specializing in student housing also know what to look for. From knob and tube wiring to wearing joists, to leaky basements, most have sold these homes more than once and are familiar with their individual characteristics, both good and bad.

They are also familiar with the unique relationships required to get financing. Regardless of how well you get along with your bank or mortgage banker, you will no doubt be surprised at their attitude toward student housing. There has been a stigma attached to student housing that major lenders simply can't get past. Even if you convince your regular lender to provide a mortgage you'll find that they want a higher down payment, will charge a higher interest rate, and will want to appraise the house as a single family dwelling (which is always lower than its value as a student home investment).

Many buyers end up using second tier banks, mortgage brokers specializing in multi-unit housing (most are in Toronto), or specialty third-party private financing. Rates, of course, are always higher than the standard bank rate, and they will likely want 30-50% down. As an investment vehicle, you will need at least 20% even if your bank deigns to work with you.

And again, even if you've received favourable mortgages and down payment levels with other real estate investment properties, student housing will require minimum 20%, no matter who you are.

Agents specializing in this vehicle have brokers and private lenders in their pocket and can hook you up with them. You would be hard pressed to find better terms.

And finally, at least for the moment, hiring an agent to buy a student house costs you nothing... zero.... nada. The Seller will pay their fees (something to keep in mind when you sell your student house) as well as their own agent's fees. So the question arises: Why not use an agent? It's free!

## For Sellers

Agents specializing in student housing know when to sell a home, for exactly how much, and usually have at least one or two buyers ready to look at your home. It is a very narrow market niche and there are only a handful of expert agents in Hamilton who spend enough time buying and selling student houses to know the market this well.

You need one of those agents. Their mailing lists consist of people who have been qualified (meaning they understand and have surpassed the financing challenge) are ready to buy (meaning they understand how important timing is), and are educated about and prepared to enter into bidding wars (inevitably every time).

The agent's most important asset is his/her ability to see what has sold in the area recently, and for what price. Homes similar to yours, homes with the same number of rooms, homes in similar condition, homes in the same neighbourhood, etc. are all factors the agent considers when pricing your home. And unlike any other type of real estate, the narrowness of this market niche allows him/her to pinpoint a selling price that is accurate and compelling to buyers.

Some owners venture into private selling and find themselves fighting the stigma of organized real estate. Unlike other markets, private selling has had little success in student housing for the simple reason that the private seller has nowhere near the information the agent has. As a result, price and timing is almost always wrong and access to qualified buyers is non-existent since virtually all investors are tied to an agent either in Hamilton (if they're smart) or in their hometown.

Lately, many investors have even become licensed real estate agents and, as such, are privy to all the insights, information, and listings that a regular agent is privy to. These are investors who became agents solely to assist them in their own portfolios. The only way you can compete with these investors is to hire a savvy agent yourself.

Some agents who recognize the value in long-term clients will give you, the Seller, a break when you sell your home. A lower commission rate, access to their info prior to actually listing, even ongoing assistance in filling the house with tenants just prior to listing (Most of these agents have a strong relationship with the McMaster Off-Campus Housing Desk).

A good agent will tell you what you need to repair and upgrade before you list, ensuring it will appeal to the current type of investor. On their own, a seller may spend too much money in one area--making it look nice, for example--and ignore important things like upgrading windows and roofing.

## Property Management

If you live out-of-town, you may want to consider hiring property management. Unlike regular rental housing, student housing requires a special type of person. There are two or three qualified and proven people in Hamilton who specialize in handling student housing and you'll find their costs relatively low for what they do.

At time of print, for less than $100 per month, you can hire a property manager who will collect rent, handle minor skirmishes (leaky toilets, lightbulbs, broken locks, etc.) and arrange for major work (plumbing, electrical, renovations). The latter is done after obtaining your approval, of course, and you usually receive the invoice directly; there is no additional mark-up.

Another type of property service will do the same for a percentage of the rent. Although a little more expensive, these providers usually have relationships with--or actually have on staff--contractors who will do the work at a reduced rate due to the volume of work they receive.

Both types of providers usually offer a service where they will help you find tenants each semester and this is often a
178

vital service. Finding tenants for student housing--we get into it more in the next section--is challenging because students view homes any time of day, any day of the week, any time of the year. Some will start looking months in advance, some will leave it till the last weekend. Most will do it after school hours, early on a weekend day, or late in the evening. And they don't all come together. Unless you're lucky enough to sign a group of friends right off the bat, you will be spending many hours driving back and forth to your house to show rooms to kids who will not make a decision right then and there. You may hear from them again or you may not. When they find a room they like, they sign up and never call the other landlords back saying they're not interested.

For this reason alone, the management team is priceless, though the going rate is half of the first month's rent. They have staff dedicated to showing rooms in their client's homes daily during the high seasons just before semester change. Because they represent several homes, they drag the kids around to see several rooms and usually *sell* them on one. It may be a room in your house, it may be in one of the other clients' homes. Don't see that as a negative. You're in competition with other student homes and your location, price, and condition will all play a role in the student's final decision. By having the management company handle the showings, however, you are exposing your rooms to more kids in less time.

If you are renting eight rooms for $450 per month plus utilities, then paying the management team $1800 may seem steep but remember they are also doing credit checks where possible, having leases signed, administrating move-ins, and handling those tenants once moved in. They arrange for rent payment which comes haphazardly to them and then, via one email transfer, to you.

Many of my clients, after having filling their homes once themselves, readily accept that the fee is worth it in the long run.

Of course, If the home you're buying is going to house your own child, then hopefully he has friends attending at the same time and your tenanting problem is solved. If not, consider he/she will make a perfect property manager for the duration.

Keep in mind, however, that they are still kids, still busy studying, and still looking to have fun. Looking after the house may be lower on their scale of importance than you would like it to be.

There are one or two real estate agents who will offer the service of helping you find tenants when you first buy the home. To some, it is part of the service they provide, allowing them to assure you that it can be done. As mentioned, they have relationships with McMaster Off-Campus Housing, and even know many of the students personally. Students often ask them about new properties and will switch homes based on their recommendations. The agent will not want to manage the home for you during the year but it will save you some money initially. You can always hire the property manager after the house is full. Remember, when buying your home, the agent's services are free so if they offer the service of filling your home, be sure to ask them if they will also charge you the ½ month rent fee or if they will, indeed, do it as part of their buying agent service. Keep in mind, it is a very time-consuming activity and it is not your agent's full time job. Offer them a bonus if they fill your house quickly.

# Finding Tenants

When most people consider investing in student homes, the first question they ask is, "How do you find all the tenants?" If they are experienced in rental properties, they understand the tried and true method of advertising on popular rental sites or local classifieds, maybe even holding an open house one weekend, to find renters. They sift through two or three potentials, do credit checks, employment checks, etc., set up payment systems, and ultimately approve a long-term tenant.

When faced with the fast-paced, every changing scenario of university life, however, these investors are concerned about the ongoing need to fill the homes with students.
It's not as difficult as you may think, though it can be very time consuming. If you're not hiring a property manager to handle it for you, be prepared for many a day and night driving over to the house to show a room.

By their very nature, students are not seasoned tenant material. They are young--often away from home for the first time--often unemployed, sometimes immature, and usually stressed. University life in the new millennium is

182

not at all like *Animal House*. In order to achieve success, students must attend a lot of classes at all times of day and night, study long hours when not in school, feed themselves, develop some kind of hygiene plan, and, oh yes, try to enjoy themselves.

Their schedules are all over the map and time is not something they can be frivolous with.

Which is why you'll get phone calls at 8am, 8pm, Sunday afternoons, etc., from students looking to see the room. Usually they are at the house now and want you to drop everything and come over, or at the very least, show them within the next few hours.

Sound ridiculous?

It is. But it's the way it's done. Because, if you don't drop everything and race over to the house, that student won't wait for you. They'll move to the house down the street and sign up with that landlord who did come out to show them a room.

This phenomenon occurs not because the kids are disrespectful of your time: Rather, it's because they only have pockets of time themselves to look for accommodations.

Of course, they're not all like this. Some students--especially first years with their parents--will plan ahead and book several viewings on a Saturday. You still have to work with their schedule as they're trying to line up several properties at 15-20 minute intervals, but you'll usually get a couple of days warning.

Groups of friends will often begin looking early as they are more organized and know they need to plan ahead if they hope to get 5-8 people in one home. These will call ahead and send one or two representatives of the group to check out the house. Groups are usually pickier, request discounts thinking that since they're a group, they deserve it (there is some merit to this), and often want the house even if they can't fill every room. You then have to decide whether to take a loss for the semester in order to gain the less stressful group lease, or talk them into letting you lease out the empty room(s) to strangers.

Regardless of who you end up with, however, they almost always come to you via McMaster's Off-Campus Housing Desk. This office, located in the Student Centre, runs an online search database where you can list your home for rent. The listing includes prices of rooms, what's included (utilities, furnishings, etc.), location, availability, contact info for you, and one to five photographs of the home. You buy the ad listing for approximately $30-70 per month (depending on how many photos) and can update anytime you wish (good for showing room availability).

This is the website that 99% of the students use to find accommodations. There are others including Kijiji®, Hamilton Spectator classifieds, a couple of property management exclusive sites, and the MLS®. But most of the homes listed on those venues are also listed on the McMaster website. If you are reading the digital version of this book, simply click here: <http://macoffcampus.mcmaster.ca/> for the webpage. If not, just Google® "McMaster off campus housing". The site has lots of other information for students concerning living off-campus but the far right button at top of the landing page takes you to the housing site.

Of course, some do think ahead. First years, for example, usually have parents involved, and they will book a day of showings a week or so in advance. You'll still have to work within their schedule of showings every 15-20 minutes on a

Saturday, as mentioned, but at least you'll get some warning.

Students looking to start school in September will begin looking as early as January. In fact, the Off-Campus Housing Desk hosts a Landlord Fair where you can set up a table showing your home. You can't have kids sign leases on that day (a school rule), but you can entice them to visit later. Savvy landlords offer discounts for students that show up. Some offer a sign-up bonus or a gift upon signing. Others are satisfied with building an email list of potential tenants they can chase after the fair. It usually takes place in January each year and if you contact the Housing desk, they'll send you an email invitation to join.

A large majority of students will wait till March or April to look for homes and these are the ones that come individually or in groups of two or three. Since they're not at school yet, they usually come on weekends and try to see a lot of homes in a short period of time. It is generally agreed that if you don't get them to sign the first time you see them, you likely will lose them to another home. How pushy you are depends upon your personality and your current level of frustration.

Students attending the September to May semester will request an eight-month lease. Although some inexperienced, lackadaisical, and uneducated landlords will do it, the norm is a twelve-month lease. As an investor, you need income each month. If you think you can lease empty rooms to summer students from May to August, remember there aren't as many, and they always want to pay less for the summer months. Even the school states that students will likely have to sign twelve-month leases, so it's not out of the norm. Of course the kids will always try (parents are actually worse if they're paying) as the savings to them is substantial. You simply have to explain that they can use the housing site to sub-lease for the months they're not living there but that the responsibility for full rent is ultimately theirs once they sign the lease. Because there are landlords out there who do allow eight month leases, you may lose a few potential tenants for this reason but hold your ground. The difference between an eight-month lease and a twelve-month lease is your annual profit+ in most cases.

Students attending in May are more inclined to accept the twelve-month lease as they are beginning just before summer. Most landlords have tenants signing leases from May to May, or September to September.

There is a growing number of exchange, specialty, and short-term students who need accommodations for three or four months. Some landlords have created a steady niche of these types of students but it is a ton of work for you, the landlord and often your home is not fully tenanted all year round. If you allow a four-month lease from Sept to December, who is going to take your room from Jan to May? There are very few students looking for accommodations in January. If they are, they're looking to begin the lease in May or September.

**Leases**

A word on leases.

There are several proven leases that you can find online. Be sure they adhere to the Ontario Landlord and Tenant Act (should state so on them somewhere). Try to keep them short (most are 2-4 pages) as students not only don't read them, but much of what is in the longer versions is actually written in the Landlord/Tenant Act and simply referring to the Act will incorporate all that legalese. If you hire a lawyer to create one for you, it will be long, incomprehensible, and expensive. It is not necessary.

Keep in mind that most of your tenants are not fully-functioning, responsible adults yet. They don't understand the ramifications of signing or breaking a lease and usually don't read them. What you need included is:

1)      name of tenant and contact info (especially email)
2)      home address and parent's names and contact info
3)      address of your house
4)       you listed as landlord with contact info
5)       price of the room and when payment is due
6)      the dates the lease is in effect
7)      who pays which utilities and how it is divided
8)      refer to Landlord/Tenant Act and all its provisions
9)      guarantor, if you can get it
10)     signatures from each tenant, you, and witnesses (can be their friend or another tenant), and dated

That's about it. Everything else legal is covered in the Act (damages, breaking leases, repairs, etc.)

Because of Hamilton's bylaw about single family housing, most landlords provide one master lease which covers the generic parts of the agreement. They then have a *Schedule A* for every tenant depicting individual information and room pricing. Each tenant then receives a copy of the master lease along with their own Schedule A. This constitutes a single lease, thereby adhering to the single family housing bylaw, though each tenant is only aware of their own commitment.

Each tenant needs a copy of the Master lease and their schedule but they do not need the schedules belonging to other tenants. You, however, do need a copy of everything. If the City requires you to present a lease for the home, you will have one lease with several Schedules attached. If this sounds confusing, feel free to email me and I'll explain further and send you a copy of the lease my clients use. (*contact info on last page*).

## Down Payment

When a student shows interest in a room in your home, the most important thing you can do is get the down-payment. This is usually the last month's rent. Don't worry about them signing a lease right away; remember they often don't fully appreciate its value or importance. What they *do* understand is money. Once they have handed over $400+ to you in cash, certified cheque, or money order, you both know they have committed to your room. It is not uncommon for a student to sign a lease with you, find a home they like better later, and sign a lease with another landlord. Who has the rights to the tenant? The person who has the down payment. Money has to change hands for a contract to be viable and getting that money is the most important thing you can do initially. You can arrange to meet at a later date to sign a lease or even leave it till the first day of school when they come up with the first month's rent. The bottom line is that if they give you the money... they're coming. If they don't, they forfeit the down payment and you lease the room to someone else. If a student asks for their down payment back, you can decide to be nice and do so, or you can keep it because technically they consolidated an agreement even though they may or may not have signed a lease yet. You are within your rights to do either. If it happens early enough in the year and you have time to find another tenant, I suggest you give them the money back. Your home's reputation is worth more than a few hundred dollars extra you will make off an unsuspecting and inexperienced student.

Don't accept personal cheques for obvious reasons. Kids write cheques with abandon and sometimes they don't clear the bank. Insist on guaranteed funds for the down payment. If they want to pay monthly rent via email transfer, credit card, cheque, etc., after that, it's up to you to decide. My clients mostly work with email transfer and lately--with products like Square®--they also accept credit card and debit card payments. Post-dated cheques are not as common and don't offer any kind of guarantee anyway. They can still bounce.

Be ready to allow a leeway of two or three days for students who are paying their own way. Some have part-time jobs with paycheque dates that don't coincide with first of the month. You will sometimes have to wait a few days for rent because of this. Don't fret, it's common. Of course, if Mom and Dad are paying, you are not as concerned and accepting twelve post-dated cheques should be safe.

Student Housing

# Chapter Five:
# Reno's and Upgrades

# What are the laws and the process?

## Permits

Officially, the City of Hamilton requires that you obtain a permit to do any renovations in your home. And, of course, that must be our official line also. Reality, however, is a little different.

No one wants to blatantly break the law. But because the law is flexible when it comes to home renovations, most investors feel they have no alternative but to try and accomplish their goals without obtaining permits.

At the very least, reno's will be completed and life will go on as normal. At worst, the City will hear of your project and come out to inspect. Almost invariably, they will post a *stop work* order on the front of the door and you or your contractor must immediately stop renovations until the City is satisfied that you are doing it properly. Most of the compliance officers who come out to your home are easy to get along with and, contrary to popular belief, are not trying to stop you from improving your home. They will take note of what you are doing, ask you and your contractor questions, and file a report. When you go to get a permit, these notes are considered and the Building Department at City Hall decides how they would like you to handle the project. In almost every case, you will need drawings but hopefully you have some kind of drawing your working with anyway, even if it's just yours. Most of the time, the City will accept your drawing and request that you do additional things that your drawing doesn't cover.

For example, if you are moving stairs, they may require an engineer to sign off on your drawings to ensure safety. Even if your contractor assures you that they are doing it to code, the City will often demand that a professional engineer agree and place their stamp on your drawings. Hiring an engineer is not cheap. Permits are not usually expensive but they do take an excessively long time to arrive.

If a compliance officer places a stop order on your home while you are renovating, count on a minimum of 3-4 weeks for you to satisfy the Building Dept. and obtain permits that allow you to move ahead. If the City has any concerns at all, that time period can extend to one or two months.

This is why some investors obtain permits first, ensuring that work won't stop. The problem with that approach, however, is that once you have closed on your home, you will still have to wait several weeks before you obtain permits, and all that time, your home sits empty, and the mortgage payments rack up. Doing it ahead of closing is difficult because of the complication of access until you own the home. Most offers only incorporate one or two visits prior to closing.

This is why other investors decide to take a chance, and start work before they get permits. In days gone by, the risk was heavy fines, denial of permits, and requests to demolish everything done to date. That doesn't happen anymore. The City has been charged by the province to improve and create accessible and affordable housing. If you are increasing rentable accommodations, or better yet, adding rentable accommodations, then the province is behind you; the City must allow you to do so. They can, of course, insist that you do it their way, which isn't always the only way, or the only safe way, and almost never the cheapest way. But they can no longer stop you, which means they cannot charge you with breaking any laws either, as long as you are willing to comply.

It's the old adage: "beg forgiveness rather than ask permission" in action. Because the City can only force you to comply to building, safety and fire codes, they cannot make you tear down your reno's as long as you can prove that they do comply.

Take photographs of every stage of your reno, showing what the home looked like before, during, and after your reno's. That way, they won't ask you to tear down walls to see what's behind them. And most importantly, be sure you or your contractor are, in fact, building to code (fire and building). If your contractor is licensed, then their reputation with the City is on the line and they will ensure work is up to code. If your contractor is not licensed, this doesn't mean they can't do work up to code but it does mean you must insist that they do so. Many unlicensed contractors will do work cheaply by cutting corners which they feel comfortable with but may not be compliant with current codes. That doesn't make them bad guys necessarily--especially if you asked them to do it as cheap as possible--but they are risking your investment by not guaranteeing you that their work would pass a City inspection.

It is the landlord that doesn't adhere to code who gives all investors a bad name. They try to do things as cheap as possible, cutting corners everywhere. They don't install proper sized windows; they don't upgrade electrical wiring; they don't improve plumbing to accommodate multiple tenants. They often aren't aware of what the codes require, and as a result, their homes are unsafe and non-compliant. It is these landlords that make the headlines when they are levied with heavy fines and refused permits.

A conscientious and honest investor will want the home to be up to safety and fire standards. These are young people in your home. They may or may not be aware of what is right and what isn't. It is your responsibility, as a landlord, to ensure that the living space is, in fact, compliant with current building and fire codes. Actually, the cost of doing it right is not that much more than doing it wrong anyway. Especially if the City makes you change everything after the fact.

I have clients who have built walls, improved electrical and plumbing, changed windows, etc., and have been stopped part way through the renovation. They have adhered to the

City's request for drawings, inspections, etc., and within 2-3 weeks, have obtained permits. This is because they were doing the renovations properly to start with. The only thing they didn't do is get the permit first (too time consuming and costly). But they were compliant to all the regulations so when inspected, the homes passed with little or no changes.

Does it sound like we are advocating not getting permits? Of course, we cannot do that in print. All we can do is provide the information as witnessed over the past ten years or so, along with relaying experiences from other landlords. You, the investor, should get advice from your agent, lawyer, contractor, and even the City itself. Then weigh the pro's and con's and make the decision that works for you. The risk in bending the rules is not as black and white as it used to be.

## Upgrades vs. Renovations

The grey area between the black and white of the law is the difference between an upgrade and a renovation.

An upgrade is when you improve upon something that exists already. For example, if your home has a dated kitchen in the basement and you modernize it, that's an upgrade.

If your home doesn't have a kitchen in the basement and you put one in, that's a renovation.

There are bylaws that stipulate that you cannot have a kitchen in the basement. But there is also new provincial legislation that states anyone can put an apartment in their basement--including a kitchen.

Who interprets what's right, not quite right, or blatantly wrong?

The City.

Do they have written instructions showing investors the difference?

Not really. And it changes constantly anyway.

The frustration only occurs when you and the City disagree on how you interpret said laws. But they don't always win, so don't be discouraged. If you can prove to the City that what you are doing is, in fact, an upgrade, then they will concede and you won't be required to obtain a renovation permit. Your upgrade will still need to pass inspection, but once again, if your intent was to do everything to code anyway, your work will pass inspection. If you cut corners, then shame on you, you deserve to be stopped. Although building and safety codes may seem excessive at times, they are the considered opinions of experts in the field and are law. Even if you disagree, you'll never prove that to any court. Adherence to the codes is the price you must pay to be able to play in this market. Anything less is irresponsible.

Sermon over.

If you're not sure what you propose to do in your home is an upgrade or renovation, the best way to find out is to do a simple drawing, show a photograph of what exists now, and ask the Building Department for an official decision. You risk that if they decide what you are doing is a renovation, then you have just *flagged* your home, meaning an inspector will no doubt pay a visit in a week or so to see if you did, in fact, adhere to policy. On the other hand, if they decide it is an upgrade, then you may continue in the knowledge that your risk factor for forced compliance was just reduced to zero. Your project may still be flagged and a compliance officer may still come out to see that your upgrades are up to code, but permits will not be part of the equation.

## A note on *flagged* homes.

If you've never heard the term before, it simply means that when your home is *flagged* it is now on the radar, meaning the City is aware you are doing something to change your home.

If a neighbour calls the City to complain about the noise your making when renovating, your home will be flagged.

If a tenant calls the City wondering why you are turning a living room into a bedroom, your home will be flagged.

If you have a large dump bin in the driveway, or if you have a lot of demolition material in your driveway or back yard, your home will be flagged.

If a contractor's vehicle is parked in your driveway for any great length of time, your home will be flagged.

If you request permission to add a parking space at the front or rear of your home, it will be flagged.

Hamilton works on a complaint-based system. There simply aren't enough compliance officers on staff to drive around town looking for renovators doing things without permits. So when a home is brought to their attention, for any of the above reasons, it will be put on a list and a compliance officer will visit within the next week or so. If they see that renovations are in progress and, when they check City records, find that no permits have been issued for the address, then they will slap a *stop work order* on the front door. If you or your contractor are at the home, they will go through your project with them on the spot. If not, they will leave a number for you to call and you will need to meet with the officer, at your home, usually within 48 hours, to discuss your project.

If your intention is to work on the home without obtaining permits, then you need to be conscious of anything that can flag your home. Some see this as being sneaky and irresponsible. Others see it as efficient and merely bending of the rules. The final decision is entirely up to you but keep in mind that since the province has dictated that affordable housing become a priority for the future, rules and regulations will not only become flexible, but may actually change, albeit slowly, in time.

## Reno Costs

When you first purchase a student residence, the initial reno's may be obvious. If it was not well-managed, it probably needs a good paintjob throughout. If you had a home inspection done, then you will also know what items need to be repaired immediately in order to be up to code and safe. Other things, like condition of windows, will be a personal decision. If the tenants are paying the utilities, then your investment is not risked by having heat escape through old, single pain windows. However, if you really care about your tenants (and their meagre finances) you may want to consider upgrading them, though it is unquestionably an expensive endeavour.

The most important rooms in the student house are the bathrooms and the kitchen. Bathrooms need to function well and should have heavy-duty vanities and fixtures. Everybody in the house will use these rooms daily and the wear and tear will be surprising. As an aside, if the plumbing has never been upgraded, you may want to consider replacing pipes with wider ones. Residential homes were not designed to house 8-10 people and so the plumbing pipes used were usually of a small calibre. But when multiple students are showering twice a day, you'll find the sewage back-ups, reduced hot water availability, and clogged drainage very real possibilities. Purpose built multiple family homes are usually built with wider piping to accommodate the heavier usage. Have a home inspector or plumber look at the piping servicing the home and get good advice on whether it will be in your best interests to upgrade to pipes that can handle the heavier load. You are responsible for plumbing inside the house and up to about 15' from the roadway. The City is responsible for the pipes leading from the municipal sewer system to the connection for your home (usually somewhere in the front yard). Many homes in Hamilton were also originally built with lead piping and if it is not damaged in any way, is not a safety issue. However, if you do any upgrading inside the house, and connect it to the City's portion, you will have to get the City out to change out the lead piping. They will do their portion at their cost but your portion could range from $5,000-$10,000. You can often tell which homes have had either lead piping replaced, or expanded piping installed, by the patch of newer asphalt on the road directly in front of the home.

## Bathrooms

Regardless of what some female students will tell you, bathtubs are not a necessity in a student home. Everyone showers, sometimes more than once a day, so having a shower stall for every three-four tenants makes sense. Some landlords have added extra shower facilities in the basements of their homes where space can't be used for anything else. (Many of the homes on King and Sterling Streets, for example, have low ceilings and are not suitable for multiple bedrooms. They do, however, lend themselves to one or two separate shower facilities.) If your home has only two bathrooms (upstairs and main floor) but most of the bedrooms are upstairs, then consider putting in an additional bathroom in the basement. Students don't mind traipsing downstairs if it means they don't have to wait for a shower, or worse yet, for the water to get hot again.

If your water heater is rented, call up the supplier and request a larger capacity one. Some owners are installing the new tankless water heaters. They are smaller (which can come in handy in basements where every inch counts) and offer instant hot water.

Although IKEA, JYSK and similar stores offer inexpensive vanities and fixtures, most landlords find that they are replacing them too often due to the constant usage. Better to install higher quality, heavy-duty and non-frilly units that can withstand the constant use.

Don't put cupboards in the bathrooms. Students will fill them with toiletries and the problem of who owns what becomes an issue, not to mention how messy half-filled bottles become. Better to have the students bring their toiletries with them each time.

## Kitchens

The large majority of students don't use the oven for cooking; most don't know how. Some cultures, of course, are strong on cooking (Asian, Indian, Eastern Europe, Caribbean, etc.), and if your students are from said cultures then the kitchen will get much more use. Cleanliness becomes the most important issue. If you have international students at your home, visit more often and try to instill the necessity of clean up and safe storage, as it can become a major problem for both others in the home, future tenants, and of course, the general health of all tenants.

The majority of students, however, either don't have time to cook, or are masters of the microwave. Quick-heat foods sell tremendously well in the two grocery stores close to McMaster. So much so that both have special aisles devoted to this type of food. Pizza shops in the surrounding area do very well, as do to a lesser extent, Chinese, Thai, and Vietnamese restaurants, fish and chip shops, and fast food franchises.

Microwaves are far more important than stoves; in fact, having two in the kitchen is not a bad idea. If the oven is used, it is virtually never cleaned so either put this on your monthly to-do list, hire a cleaner monthly, or plan on replacing the stove every year or so. (Surprisingly, a lot of owners do the latter which has sparked a small cottage industry in downtown Hamilton for cheap, used appliances).

Students are used to having one cupboard which they call their own. Some owners will label cupboards to match room numbers. Similar sharing takes place in the refrigerator. If you have more than five students in your home, consider a second fridge. Do not allow tenants to have bar fridges, microwaves, hotplates, or window air conditioners in their rooms. Other than being against code and a real fire hazard in most cases, such items will increase utility costs dramatically. Even if the tenants are paying utilities, it will be unfair to those who do not have extra units in their rooms.

Kitchens are often the common area in many homes meaning it is the only place in the home where all the tenants congregate. Buy a decent table and chairs for your tenants. Put up a chalkboard/pin board where you can post notices and they can post chore schedules. If it is the only common room in the house, consider hanging a television on one wall. Remember, you're not supplying television service, just a conduit for video games or large screen monitor for tenant usage in a group study setting. (Be sure the TV has an HDMI plug in setting.)

If you have a living room as an additional common area, then that is where a TV, couch, coffee table and extra chairs will go but for the most part, kids like hanging around the kitchen.

The flooring should be inexpensive laminate or linoleum. If it already has ceramic, don't change it but don't replace the above with ceramic as it is harder to clean and chips easily with heavy wear.

There is some argument among landlords, property managers, and school staff that the more modern, new and clean a kitchen is, the better quality tenant you will attract. It is hard to argue this point as it would seem to be common sense. But do you, as an investor, spend money upgrading a functional kitchen to make it more modern? The cost (between $3-5,000) may be hard to justify, especially if the current kitchen is working. If it's old, change the cupboard doors and handles. Paint the cupboards. Change the flooring. Whatever it needs to appear fresh and clean. But modern kitchens are lost on most students. Though they may have enjoyed such luxuries at home, they don't expect them in their school accommodations.

The few landlords I know who have upgraded their kitchens do, indeed attract older, more conscientious students, or in some cases first year students whose parents really want their kids to live in an environment that resembles home life. But the target market is smaller and when landlords make a mistake and pick a not-so-conscientious tenant, their costly upgrades get ruined fairly quickly and repairs become considerably higher. (Keep in mind that once Mom and Dad go home, the first year student may not be as concerned about the standard of living he/she has now adopted as their parents are.)

## Resale

When thinking about selling your home, think about the things that concern you when you are shopping. Homes with new roofs, fresh, modern kitchens and bathrooms, freshly painted rooms with laminate flooring. These are all things that make a house stand out from the rest. If you know the roof is old but it isn't causing any problems, why not budget for it but do it just before you sell. Bathrooms and kitchens are tougher because they are used all the time and it cannot be said with any kind of guarantee that a new kitchen will increase the value of the house. Most investors buy a home based on its potential income, not its appearance. Sure, if repairs are blatantly obvious, the owner has done themselves a disservice by putting it on the market in poor condition. The marketplace will bring the price down and the owner will eventually sell at that lower price. However, if the home is in an ideal location and has a large number of rooms, some of those repairs will be overlooked.

And if two or more people agree, that house will go into a bidding war and the owner will get more than list price. A lot of it is timing. When selling a student house, the time of year and the existence of current or future leases are critical; much more so than the aesthetics.

If there are a lot of homes similar to yours on the market and you have an updated bath and kitchen, then yours will likely sell first... but not necessarily for more money.

Upgrading windows, furnace, A/C, etc. are all things you look for when buying a student home but most don't offer these items. Most student homes have original windows (or just some have been updated); older, often original furnaces; and non-existent A/C. If you choose to add these when you own the house, then hopefully you acquired it for a good price because those are costly items, which is precisely why many owners don't perform them.

In order to be compliant with current safety code, of course, means that some of the things in a student home should be replaced immediately. Some investors aren't as concerned about being compliant as others but when it comes to the safety of the students, and your own peace of mind, compliance is essential. Therefore, egress windows in each basement bedroom will be needed if windows are still original. When many of these homes were built, they incorporated small, slider windows which would not allow a person to climb out of. Larger windows (which may result in the digging out of a window trench) in each bedroom is the minimum needed for code. Some argue that the code requires only two exits from the basement area; one being the main side door, the other an egress window in the living room or kitchen. In fact, we have seen enough compliance investigators insist on egress windows in every bedroom because most tenants lock their bedroom doors despite that being illegal also. Local fire departments agree that although not specified in code, the City would enforce such a requirement upon investigation.

## Permits

Yes, you should, by law, obtain permits for all renovations prior to beginning work. In reality, however, most owners do not. The gray area that suggests much of what you are doing is upgrading allows that a permit is not required. For example, if you are updating a kitchen or bathroom, you wouldn't need a permit. But if you are adding a bathroom, you do. Likewise, for altering a living room to become a bedroom: Although no structural changes are being made, a permit would be required.

The City wants to work with student landlords and tries to make the process simple when applying for permits. If the home has been a student residence in the past, and all you are doing is upgrading to make it safer, cleaner, more modern, etc., then you will have no problem. If you are trying to add rooms (Living room/dining room; basement) then the requirements get a little hazy. You will need architectural drawings and will need to adhere to full multi-unit housing fire and safety codes. This includes putting fire resistant insulation between floors; replacing regular doors with fire doors at exits; putting egress windows in all bedrooms; hardwiring a fire alarm system; and more.

That's why some investors start the work prior to obtaining a permit. The reason (other than cost)? Because if you are caught part-way through a renovation, then there is some argument as to whether what you are doing is upgrading, not renovating, since no one knows what was there before. It's a tricky fence-walking attitude and doesn't always work out for the owner. There are penalties on the books as much as $25,000 in fines for running an illegal lodging house. But

216

this has never been enforced in the McMaster area (some in the Eastern and Central Hamilton area). Your assessment of the risk is what will determine which way to choose to go. Get advice from other owners and your real estate agent prior to deciding. You will then have the experiences and opinions of those who have done it both ways. If you get advice from your lawyer or the City, expect that they will insist on compliance prior to renovation.

## Tenant Expectations

When renting to a student, it is important to know what they consider important aspects of your lease.

Primarily, they want the internet. Schooling is virtually impossible today without a strong, fast, reliable internet connection. They do a lot of studying at home, sometimes with friends in their rooms and a strong, fast signal is a must.

They would also prefer that it be free. Cogeco provides a service whereby you can cap how much internet is used in your home to $100 per month at time of print. For most students' homes, this suffices. If you find they are complaining, it's because they want to download movies (remember you don't provide cable TV service), or watch YouTube® videos all night. Neither of this is necessary to schooling so don't feel bad if you don't provide an expensive internet service to accommodate this.

Bell does not provide a cap service and bills can go as high as several hundred dollars per month. If your students are paying utilities, then this doesn't matter to you… until they stop paying the bill.

There are other third party internet providers who offer a good service for a low price. But they come and go frequently. If you're interested in trying one out, ask the students; they are always on top of the best provider in the area.

Next to internet, the kids want to have access to a kitchen, a shower, and a clean room. And that's about it. A large majority don't cook much so a microwave is essential. The more showers you have the better

A clean room consists of a bed, desk, dresser drawers and plenty of floor space for throwing dirty clothes. And, of course, all of that is their responsibility (unless you advertise that you'll provide furnishings).

Security is also becoming more of an issue these days. Many parents (especially first years) want to know what kind of security you have on entrances and room doors. Although technically illegal in Hamilton, every bedroom usually has a locking door with only two keys. You get one and the tenant gets one. Front doors are usually single lock doors and there should be no inside padlock for obvious reasons.

There have been no major security issues in the area for many years but minor theft is regularly reported. Usually, it's a student in the house stealing from another student and there's not much you can do about it as long as you provide a good lock on the entrances. It's up to the students to keep their room doors locked.

While selling a student home, the liability insurance your real estate agent carries covers any losses that can be proven while visitors are viewing the rooms. I haven't heard of an agent or client ever stealing a student's items but it is something you can say to the tenants to assure them that leaving their doors open during viewings is acceptable during the selling process.

The Landlord/Tenant Act lays out all the stipulations for the right to have quiet space, unhindered use of the home, uninterrupted use of the home (until you give them 24 hours notice of any visit, including those by you). If other tenants are not honouring those stipulations, then they should be removed. Doing so is a long, tedious process, and you'll likely lose other tenants during the process, but as mentioned before, it is a rare occurrence. School requires so much time, study and effort that most 2nd year and onward are too busy studying to become difficult tenants.

Some students expect that you, the Landlord, will provide similar services their parents do. Notes posted in the kitchen, along with welcoming package or discussion upon arrival will alleviate any confusion here.

The tenants are expected to keep the house clean, dishes done, bathrooms cleaned, and garbage taken out weekly. It is up to them to establish a schedule for all tenants to adhere to. If you find your home is not being looked after, then step in and provide a schedule depicted who does what, when. Then check back in a couple of weeks to see if it is being adhered to.

Some landlords hire a cleaning service to come in monthly and raise the rent accordingly. It's not a bad idea as long as it doesn't take your rent out of reach. In most cases, however, the kids may have lapses now and again, but when it gets really bad, someone usually steps up to the plate and does a little cleaning.

Students will also ask if they can be a couple of days late on rent upon occasion. It's up to you how to handle this. Just understand that if Mom and Dad aren't paying, then the student is likely working part-time to cover rent and paycheques don't always coincide with the first of the month. Of course, they should budget, but many are on their own for the first time and haven't learned that skill yet. Occasional leniency will ensure happy tenants.

When first arriving at your home, students may request to come in a week or so earlier than their lease commencement date. If the room is empty, I suggest you let them. They hit the ground running at school and that extra time is invaluable. Of course, if you have a tenant in the room, then they don't legally have to vacate until the end of the day their lease states. This should be the day before the new lease begins. (For example, many kids begin a semester May 1st. The other tenants should be out by midnight April 31st) I suggest you be available, if not on site, on semester change overs to ensure there is no animosity between students who are leaving and those arriving. The school is not beyond having a final exam on the last day of semester, leaving the student no time to pack and leave by the last day. They are sometimes moving in the morning of the next semester start. If you know of this ahead of time, you can ask the new student to arrive later in the afternoon. Some students are even willing to store items in the garage a day or two ahead of time (a weekend usually) if they can't move in on the exact date.

**Other items that may come up are:**

Utensils/dishes/cookware: Do you provide or do they bring them in?

I suggest you provide them initially, allowing the students to bring in their own personal items. Cookware is something they will likely not think of until they arrive. It is also a tremendous selling point when trying to rent rooms. Don't buy expensive items though as it is sometimes easier to replace damaged cookware than repair or clean misused ones. IKEA is the ideal place to find supplies for the kitchen. For less than $60-80 you can supply your home with all the items the students will need in the kitchen. Even if you do that each semester, it's a small price to pay for the ongoing happiness of the tenants.

*(Minor note: When selling a vacant house, supplying new cookware that is visible can often be a strong selling point*

Student Housing

*to a new owner. Though small in cost, it indicates your attention to detail.)*

Finally, whatever your lease depicts at the beginning of the term, that is what is expected for the duration. For example, you cannot renovate during the term of the lease unless you acquire written permission from each tenant. You cannot change the layout of the home during a lease (i.e.: change a living room to a bedroom), without written agreement from all tenants. And you cannot enter the home without giving each tenant 24 hours notice. That notice can be placed on the front door. You do not need a reply or confirmation. Of course, if you develop a good relationship with the tenants, most will not mind you visiting occasionally, especially if you help them clean, fix the internet, take out excess garbage, etc.

If you have rented the home to a group of 6 friends but you have 7 rooms, unless the lease depicts your right to lease that extra room to a stranger, you cannot do so. You need to discuss this up front with the group and put it in writing. Many students don't want to live in multi-room houses and will pay more to be in a four or five-room home. Others enjoy the comradery of a large group-even if they weren't friends at first-and look for the larger homes. The size of your home will be dependent upon your anticipated return and, of course, the price you paid. Regardless, tenant expectations are the same.

Student Housing

# Chapter Six:
# Selling a Student Home

## Why are student homes treated differently?

At some point you will want to sell your student home. Unlike other properties, residential or commercial, student homes need to be handled in a little differently. This is not the time to try to do it alone. You will need an agent. Why?

Because student homes are sold to investors and virtually all serious investors use an agent (some are agents themselves). An agent has access to all the listings as soon as the homes become available. As many homes go into bidding wars--sometimes within 24 hours--it is vital they have this information quickly.

Agents specializing in student homes usually have mailing lists of investors who are looking to buy and your home may fit their bill. Some agents will even do private deals (only one agent involved) if this happens as there would be no need to advertise on the MLS®.

If you think Buyers drive around the neighbourhood and call all the brokerages with signs on the front lawns of the homes, you'll miss out because many owners don't put up signs; it makes tenants nervous and insecure. The Toronto and Hamilton real estate boards are very strong when it comes to promoting student homes and the language used in listing descriptions-both public and board--clearly depicts the type of investment. Savvy investors know what to look for, online.

There are also considerable legal issues to contend with (i.e.: leases, first and last month's rent, etc.) and liabilities that specialists can make you aware of without you having to pay a lawyer for the same information. Some agents even deal with tenant issues separately, once a deal is negotiated, in order to keep legal costs down; all as part of their commissioned service. They have concluded many deals of this nature and are well versed in the requirements as well as the liabilities. Lawyers have been known to complicate this aspect of the deal, making both sides apprehensive. It also adds cost and since all leases are short term (8-12 months), there is no need for extensive liability clauses.

The Landlord Tenant Act clearly states how tenants should be treated during a transition. Things like honouring existing leases, ensuring no repairs/upgrades/renovations are performed during a lease tenure (unless accepted by all tenants in writing), respecting the twenty-four-hour notification rule, etc. If you don't want to read the very lengthy document, just have your agent cover the highlights so you don't do anything you shouldn't do.

Transfer of ownership in student homes can be accomplished without the owner ever meeting the tenants, if that is your preference. Hire a management company and let them and your agent work out the details of occupancy, maintenance, rent collection, etc. It is not common but there are homes where students and owners never meet; everything is handled initially by the agent, and then upon closing, the management company takes over.

# How to price and promote

Again, this is where an agent becomes indispensable. Prices of student homes vary from zone to zone (although not as much as they used to). Condition of the home obviously makes a difference (though again, not as much as in the past).

And number of available rooms and vacancy rate are critical. Savvy investors will be looking for minimum seven bedrooms. If your home has more, great. If it has less, then you need to price accordingly. Many student homes with 5 and 6 rooms have languished on the market simply because they were overpriced. Their owners (and perhaps their agents) didn't understand that regardless of location and/or condition of the home, if it doesn't have the potential to bring in an acceptable ROI, it won't interest an investor. On the other hand, parents with children attending McMaster often don't want large homes and are interested in 4-6 bedroom homes (enough for their child and a couple of his/her friends).

Agents specializing in student housing are watching the market daily and they will tell you that pricing changes with each semester. They will also tell you that marketing to a family (those with children attending school), and marketing to an investor are two completely different activities. Investors look at numbers. Parents look at condition, location, and then the numbers. As long as Johnny or Sally can live in the home for free (their friends will pay all expenses for the home, even if rent is discounted), then parents are usually happy. The bonus of value appreciation doesn't usually dawn on them until graduation when they realize that the kids not only lived in town free but the investment has also made an amazing profit (one of the main reasons some hang onto them even when the children have moved on).

Your agent will look at what comparable homes have sold for in the immediate area over the past semester or so and have a pretty accurate idea of what your house is worth. Number of rooms, any existing leases, location, and condition of the home, will all be factors taken into account when choosing a list price. You will then add $10-15,000 to allow for negotiating (no investor or parent pays list price, ever).

Number of rooms, location, and existing leases will be far more important to buyers than condition of the home. Currently, homes in the $400-$450,000 range still boast original flooring, Formica countertops, and retro-cabinets. Many kitchens, appliances, bathrooms, furnaces, etc. are original and we're talking about an area where the average home is 50-70 years old. These homes in any other part of Hamilton would be valued at $100-$200,000 less.

## Promotion

Again, this is your agent's domain. There are buyers looking for student homes every day. They don't look in newspapers, magazines, or newsletters. They are receiving notifications (usually via email) from their agents every time a new house comes up on the market. Agents specializing in the field regularly contact investors when a particularly good home pops up.

You want to be part of that circle. Listing on the MLS® is not enough. Student home investors want to filter out other types of homes; they are only interested in multiple-room properties. The MLS® does not distinguish rooms in basements in a public search. Most student homes show up as 2 or 3 bedroom properties. That's because the other 3-4 rooms are in the lower level.

Buyers also want to know the numbers. Give your agent all the info, let them do a Profit and Loss sheet (including potential income), and email that to their mailing list. If the numbers work, you'll get tons of showings.

On average, for every ten showings, you'll get one offer. If you price the house properly (perhaps $5,000 below value), you'll get those first ten showings within 24 hours and be sold before the weekend (when everyone else shows up). Usually though, you'll get 20 or more showings and you'll be enjoying a bidding war. Remember, student housing is usually a seller's market. There aren't enough homes to service all the buyers looking to invest. It's virtually a feeding frenzy every time a good property comes up. If a student house languishes on the market for more than two weeks, then it's overpriced. It doesn't matter what the condition, location, number of rooms, etc. is... if the price matches the value, it will sell; there are simply too many buyers out there looking for it not to.

Once you set your price, visit all the competitive houses nearby at a similar price. Be objective. If you were buying, which house would you choose? If the problem is the condition of the house, then either fix the problem, or lower the price.

If you think you don't have enough rooms, lower the price to match other homes with similar number of rooms, regardless of location. And if you can afford to undercut the competition by $5,000, do so, because your house will sell first.

# The secret to getting top dollar

Empty or Full?

Much debate occurs as to whether you should sell your home with leases intact, or with all tenants gone. There are good arguments for both sides. If you think your home will appeal to a parent, then it should be empty. If you think it's more for an investor, then ensure you have 12-month leases at top dollar (your agent will tell you what that number should be).

If the home needs work, and you've priced accordingly, it's better to be empty so the buyer can come in immediately and begin reno's. Remember, if there are tenants living in the home when you sell it, the buyer must honour those leases, by law. So they can't start any reno's until those tenants are gone. And tenants have the right to remain, even after the lease is concluded, reverting to a month-to-month status and a restricted rent increase. (Read the Landlord/Tenant Act if you're not sure how that works).

If you have a seven bedroom plus home, then you will appeal to investors and you may be better off having the house full, with leases signed, and happy tenants ready to stay on. Of course, this brings us to the other contested issue: timing.

If you're home will appeal to a parent, then you should understand that those folks are usually looking for a home well in advance of semester start. Students start in either May or September (the majority in the latter month) and first year students usually receive their letter of acceptance sometime in February or March. Mom and Dad are already looking by then (though perhaps only on the MLS® until the final choice of university is made). Once that happens, they usually find an agent immediately and begin actively shopping. Some are pro-active and hook up with a local specialist agent, whereas others use their own agent in their own town. Often they become discouraged with the latter (because they can't possibly have the knowledge and accessibility local agents do) and hire a specialist later. Either way, they are looking at homes as early as January. Parent investment homes take longer to sell (as they often don't appeal to investors due to price, lack of rooms, price due to proximity to campus, etc.), so listing right after Christmas isn't a bad idea.

Likewise, for the September starters (the majority of students), June and July become shopping months also, though not as strong as spring time. If your home needs some upgrades/reno's allow for that and list earlier in the year. Some parents will begin looking for homes in March and April even if their children aren't attending until September. Once their child gets the school's acceptance letter, they are ready to shop.

If you strongly feel your home will appeal to an investor (perhaps you're an investor yourself, not a parent), then the best time to sell is February, May, late August, or October. It will make a big difference if your home is vacant or leased, of course. If you have a fully leased home, then timing is not as critical to an investor as they are looking for a turnkey operation anyway.

But if the house needs any kind of work (be brutal in your assessment here), then allow for that. Your buyer will need time not only to renovate/repair/upgrade, but also time to find tenants. The best time to sell this type of home is November/December, March, or June. These predictions are based on past history. Student houses are bought and sold every month of every year, but the idea is to time your sale to realize maximum profit. There are more student home buyers shopping in the spring, early winter, and late summer, than other times in the year. Inventory is lower during slow periods meaning your home doesn't compete as much. But there aren't as many buyers.

If your home needs work, price it properly, and it will sell anytime of year. If your house is in prime condition, then wait till the most buyers are shopping; you'll get more money. Very few bidding wars occur in the summer. Almost every home during spring experiences bidding wars. It's the sheep/wolf thing. Don't fight it. Time your sale accordingly.

Student Housing

# Chapter Seven:
# Summary and a Look Ahead

# Emerging markets

McMaster University, Columbia College and Mohawk College are all growing in size. But the City can't continue to accommodate this growth. All the schools have maximized their available land space and can't expand current campuses much more.

As a result, additional campuses have been located outside the City. At the moment, most are specialty campuses such as the Grand Erie Six Nations Clinical Education Campus - Brantford Centre in Brantford, the McMaster Health Campus in downtown Hamilton (across from City Hall), the DeGroot /Ron Joyce Business campus in Burlington, and one or two continuing education campuses also in Burlington. Even Oakville's Sheridan College has opened smaller, specialty operations in Burlington, Hamilton, and Brantford.

But very little housing has been added. Student accommodations in Burlington is virtually non-existent. The City is much stricter with their bylaws for multi-unit housing and the cost of property there is so high that investors simply can't make it work financially, even if they could operate a student house.

In fact, at time of print, the majority of students attending the Burlington campus are bussed in from the main campus on Main St. in Hamilton. Those students live in and around the main campus. This has added tremendous strain to the already languid housing shortage and there is no doubt some enterprising developer will convince Burlington council that some kind of residence is needed to fulfill the growing need there. That campus is destined to grow as there is plenty of available land nearby allowing for major expansion (You can see the campus located on the South Service Road as you pass through Burlington on the QEW).

Accommodations in Burlington and Oakville will not be suitable for the small investor looking at single units with 7-8 bedrooms as these homes would be priced too high to make any financial sense. Likely, if anything is done, it will be in the form of low-rise or even high-rise residence-type facilities built by developers, and no doubt with government subsidies or foreign investment funds.

Some residents of Burlington, Dundas, Ancaster, and Waterdown have taken advantage of new provincial laws and built basement apartments (legal or non-conforming) and lease to older students (4th year, post-grads, and beyond) who are able to drive to campus. This is a small cottage industry in itself but is limited to those who already live in the area. I have heard of one or two investors who have purchased a home, rented the upstairs to a family, and then opened one or two rooms in the basement to students, but as of print, this is not a trend I see expanding much. Again, the ROI is simply not high enough. Some investors have had more success doing this on the West Hamilton mountain (west of Upper James St.), with renters upstairs and students downstairs who attend Mohawk College. Be aware, however, that maintaining a full house twelve months a year is extremely difficult with community colleges. Most courses are one or two years in length meaning you are constantly seeking tenants. Also, the very nature of a community college means most of the students are locals. Some investors in this area of the Mountain have reverted the basements to full apartments and turned them into duplexes (legal or non-conforming), and make a better continuous ROI.

## Brantford

The Telephone City (Alexander Graham Bell is purported to have made one of the first phone calls from Brantford to Paris, Ontario from a family homestead there), is a town in transition. It has tried desperately to maintain its viability through a Casino (owned by the Natives), downtown revitalization (moderately successful), and the insurgence of students attending specialty campuses (Clinical Education Campus) and nearby Waterloo University and Wilfred Laurier University (Kitchener). Students are bussed from Brantford to the latter two campuses for classes. Small campuses have emerged in the town itself (the Faculty of Law, for example, holds classes downtown) and many social activities take place in venues in and around town.

Like many towns going through transition, there are pockets of success and havens of failure. Brantford is a prime example. When driving downtown, you will see both boarded up businesses beside regionally well-known entertainment facilities (The Sanderson Centre is in the centre of town and hosts major national acts). The core is also experiencing a summer surge of sorts with its Jazz

Festival which, though small in size, attracts fans from as far away as Toronto, Montreal, and Detroit.

With Waterloo and Kitchener experiencing a student housing dilemma over the past decade, Brantford's hospitality is a welcome change for investors. The Tri-Cities (Kitchener, Waterloo, Cambridge) councils voted for more restrictive housing rules, licensing, and an influx of foreign (mostly Chinese) investment. As a result, there are many small housing developments (low-rise apartments, residences, and multi-level boarding houses) that accommodate students. However, due to the added restrictions, licensing, etc., the cost of accommodation for students has skyrocketed, outpacing even Toronto university standards.

Developers and small investors alike are viewing Brantford as a solution waiting to happen. Students have been bussed from Brantford to Waterloo and Kitchener campuses for a few years now and that will likely continue. However, the individual student home residence phenomenon has yet to hit the town. Homes are cheaper in Brantford than in surrounding cities, and the same number of rooms can be rented out.

Logic would dictate that Brantford will become one of the next student residence meccas. In fact, some predict that major campuses will also be located here in the near future due to the availability of land and vacant property.

Again, as with transitional towns, there are some areas where suburbs thrive and house prices are rising to Hamilton levels. But other parts of town (namely older sections near the river and downtown core) are still attractive. Yes, some of these homes need major upgrades and renovations. But if the purchase price is right, and the availability of tenants is growing, then investors will find it attractive.

Forecasting future prosperity, the owner of the Brantford Expositor--the presiding local weekly newspaper--moved his operations from its downtown long term home to smaller offices nearby, and is turning the original multi-storey building into student residences.

Since McMaster University is less than forty-five minutes away, Brantford (and smaller communities between Hamilton and Brantford (Dundas, Lynden, Flamborough,

Paris) are potential sites for other campuses. Land is cheaper here than in the GTA corridor and housing that can be retro-fitted to become student accommodations are plentiful. Of course, Waterloo and Wilfred Laurier are also looking to these communities for both future campus locations as well as possible accommodation sites. As with most secondary University activities (of which housing is one), the growth and development of student accommodation in these locales will be driven by investors, not academics.

## St Catharines

Nestled just before the tourist mecca of Niagara Falls is the City of St. Catharines. Another transition town, though larger than Brantford, St. Catharines boasts two quickly growing schools: Niagara College and Brock University, the latter being located in the south-western part of the City, close to its largest shopping mall, the Pen Centre.

Brock University has moved, expanded, and grown its campuses over the past two decades until it has become a prominent player in the university arena. Established as a glorified community college, Brock has become a leader in fields such as Biological Sciences, Biotechnology, Computer Science, Mathematics, Physics, and more.

The new campus is on the outskirts of town and is surrounded by former residential suburbs built in the 1950s and 60s. Many of these homes have been retrofitted to become six to nine-bedroom student homes that rival Hamilton homes located south of Main Street. But the cost is, again at time of print, approximately $50,000-80,000 lower, making ROI much stronger as students pay similar room rates here as they do in Hamilton.

Depressed by a lagging shipping and manufacturing infrastructure (the Welland Canal begins its journey from Lake Ontario to Lake Erie in St. Catharines), much of the City's downtown core, and nearby older suburbs have been abandoned and many investors have left due to the lack of jobs and, of course, renters. The City's outlying suburbs are thriving due to its proximity to the wine vineyards in Niagara-on-the-Lake, Niagara Falls, (and related tourism spin-offs), and an upsurge in retail and university-related businesses.

Port Dalhousie, home of an annual Olympic-level rowing regatta is a suburb of St. Catharines located on the edge of

Lake Ontario and is experiencing a re-birth as a tourism destination similar to Niagara-on-the-Lake (less than five miles away). Niagara College, located in the heart of tourism country and similar in scope to Mohawk, is known for its Bachelor of Arts degree in Game Design and various culinary diploma courses which ties in nicely with the tourism-heavy Niagara Falls/Niagara-On-The-Lake locale nearby. Still a small college, its students' accommodations consist of two residences and local basement apt. facilities. But again, there are plenty of abandoned warehouses, retail space, housing, etc., to accommodate a growing student environment as well as campus operations.

## The Future

There is talk of entertainment campuses located in and around Niagara Falls and St. Catharines, as well as agricultural and geological campuses on the shores of Lake Erie. Dundas and Waterdown are growing a base of artists that could warrant the establishment of a school of creative endeavour in and around the Flamborough area. (Several national and international writers, painters, sculptors and actors hail from the area.) And McMaster has made overtures about commandeering various vacated warehouses and office complexes abandoned by the virtually defunct steel industry which created Hamilton in the first place.

Student Housing

# Conclusion

The prices of student homes have risen every year. Over the past decade or so, many of us who buy and sell these homes regularly, have waited for a cap; a level where prices couldn't go higher. We were amazed when homes broke the $400,000 mark around 2010. Early in 2016, the first $500,000 home sold.

For many investors, the ROI doesn't work anymore as rents have not kept up with rising costs of property. For others-- especially those who work appreciation into their calculations--student housing is still one of the best investments available.

Many of my clients have made 15-25% ROI on their student home investments, usually within a five-year period. One client who purchased, renovated, and sold within a six-month period, made a 75% profit. Admittedly, that doesn't happen often.

But will these same homes surpass the $600,000 mark? Probably. And likely within the next five years. The schools are constantly expanding but accommodations are not keeping up with the demand. Rents are slowly increasing noticeably as of 2014, and upon reflection, it seems that for every $100,000 in purchase price, rooms are renting for $50 higher. To some, this math works.

If you are looking for a long-term investment, a place to park your money, a tax-haven, etc., then student housing is worth a look. If you are a *flipper* then student housing likely isn't the venue for you. Family homes have been flipped successfully over the years but most of the residences have been bought up and converted. And older student homes in need of upgrading simply don't meet the criteria of a quick flip. Appreciation is a prime factor in this investment. Student homes increase in value at approximately a 35% higher rate than any other residential or multi-housing property in Hamilton, including the latest duplex craze (bungalows being turned into two-family homes).

As long as you are aware of the financial challenges; the fact that you are dealing mostly with young people away from home for the first time; that turnover is very high; and that location isn't as important as amenities; then you will do well with this investment vehicle.

As with any investment book discussing specific properties, things change over time. In order to keep the information in this book up-to-date, I encourage you to join my mailing list (email editor@robertjmorrow.com, or go to www.robertjmorrow.com and sign up for regular emails.)

As things change, I will update this book and offer free editions to those on the mailing list. I also send out regular emails concerning various issues in the Hamilton Student Home arena, as well as offering free emails of all student homes listed for sale at any given time.

If you are interested in pursuing the purchase of a student home, I would encourage you to go to www.emailhomes.ca which is my real estate site. By filling out the form on the *Contact Us* page, you'll be able to see all the student homes available, as well as any new ones that pop up while you're on the mailing list.

I have also produced several videos on various aspects of student housing in Hamilton. In each brief video, I answer the most common questions asked by investors. You can access those videos here: (If you are reading a digital version, click on the link. If you are reading the paperback, just go to YouTube and type in "student homes in Hamilton". You'll find I pretty much own the first couple of pages.)

And finally, if you have found this book informative in any way, please tell your investor friends. But more importantly, for independent writers, please go to **amazon.ca** or **amazon.com** and rate the book--perhaps even write a short review. The more reviews on file, the higher the book's ranking.

If you wish to receive updates on the book, *in the format you originally purchased*, please email me at editor@robertjmorrow.com. If you have any questions about student housing, please contact my team via robert@emailhomes.ca.

**Robert J. Morrow** *spent four decades in advertising, marketing, journalism, and publishing, prior to becoming a real estate agent. He is a member of the Canadian Real Estate Association, the REALTORS® Association of Hamilton and Burlington, and the International Association of Business Communicators. He has been a guest columnist for the industry's national magazine: REM (Real Estate Magazine), and has written two other real estate books which are available at www.amazon.ca or www.robertjmorrow.com.*

*Since specializing in 2009, Mr. Morrow has bought and sold over $15 million worth of student housing. All of his clients have made money; many still own properties and have paper profits of 100% plus.*

*Mr. Morrow divides his time between writing and real estate and lives in Dundas, Ontario, with his business and life partner,* **Susan Gogishvili***.*

Made in the USA
Lexington, KY
08 June 2019